◄SPEARHEAD►

5th GEBIRGSJÄGER DIVISION
Hitler's mountain warfare specialists

SPEARHEAD

5th GEBIRGSJÄGER DIVISION
Hitler's mountain warfare specialists

Michael Sharpe

Ian Allan PUBLISHING

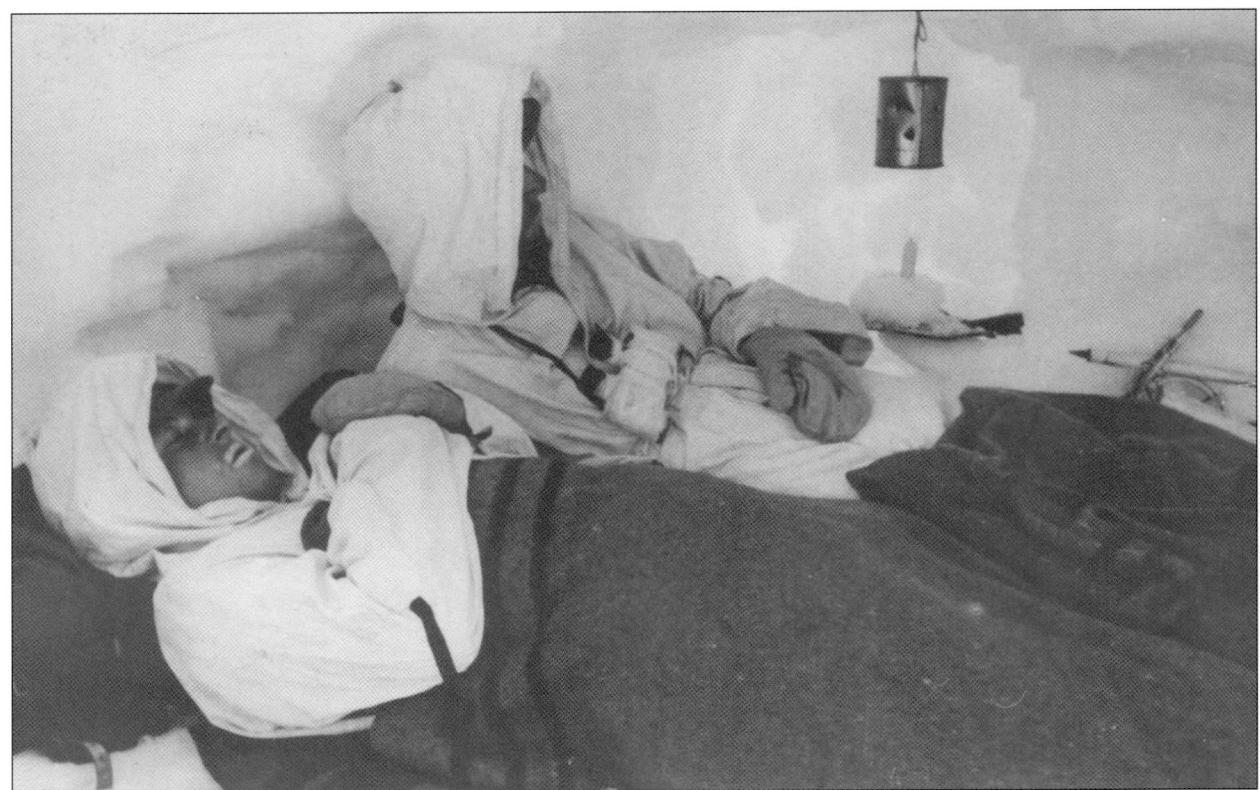

Acknowledgements
Photographs and captions via TRH Pictures and
Chris Ellis
Design: Compendium Design
Maps: Mark Franklin

Note: Internet site information provided in the Reference
section was correct when provided by the author. The
publisher can accept no responsibility for this information
becoming incorrect.

Above: Mountain troops in white two-piece winter suits bed down
in the snow on the Eastern Front. Note white cloth covering the
binoculars.

Previous page: Infantry company resting high in the mountains
while on exercise in Austria.

First published 2005

ISBN 0 7110 3045 6

© Compendium Publishing, 2005

Published by Ian Allan Publishing

an imprint of Ian Allan Publishing Ltd, Hersham, Surrey KT12 4RG
Printed in England by Ian Allan Printing Ltd, Hersham, Surrey KT12 4RG

Code: 0505/A2

British Library Cataloguing in Publication Data
A CIP catalogue record for this book is available from the British Library

CONTENTS

ORIGINS & HISTORY

From the earliest years of the Third Reich, the German military was expanded well beyond the limits placed on it by the hated Versailles 'diktat'. This expansion eventually embraced the small *Gebirgs*, or mountain, brigades within the newly organised Wehrmacht, so that at the outbreak of war there were three full *Gebirgsjäger* (mountain rifle) divisions on strength. As the war progressed further divisions were raised. By the end, Germany had fielded 19 Gebirgs divisions (11 army and 8 Waffen SS) and four *Hochgebirgs* (high mountain) battalions, although in fact, many of these were 'mountain' units in name only and, particularly within the Waffen SS, noticeably lacking in the skills of mountaincraft. The first SS mountain formation, 6th Gebirgs Division Nord, was formed in 1941 under the name Kampfgruppe Nord, but the standard of training was below that of the true mountain units and they suffered accordingly on the northern sector of the Eastern Front.

A most notable exception was the elite 5th Gebirgs Division, known also as the *Gamsbock* Division or *Sumpfjäger* Division, which was formed in the autumn of 1940 from the 100th Mountain Infantry Regiment of the 1st Gebirgs Division and elements of the 10th Infantry Division. After training in the Bavarian Alps, it first saw action during the spring of 1941 in the Balkans, where it helped crack the Metaxas defensive line and then conquer Greece. Within weeks of the successful Greek campaign, it became part of the German assault force launched against Crete. Again the unit distinguished itself, making a vital intervention at a crucial stage of the battle at Maleme and relieving the beleaguered Fallschirmjäger at Retimo.

From late summer 1941 to March 1942, the division was on occupation duty in Norway. In March 1942 it was sent to the Eastern Front, where it was attached to Army Group North and helped check the Soviet counteroffensive between Lake Ladoga and Novgorod. It remained on the Northern Front (as the northern sector of the Eastern Front is referred to here) and took part in the operations around Leningrad until the end of 1943.

In November, the 5th was withdrawn from the Russian Front and transferred to Italy under the control of the Tenth Army. It took part in the fighting retreat up the Italian mainland, distinguishing itself during the battles for the Gustav and Gothic Lines. Near the end of the war, after fighting on the Italo-French frontier, it surrendered to American forces in Turin in May 1945. During these and other actions the division established for itself an enduring reputation for bravery and professionalism that places it among the foremost units in military history.

ORIGINS OF THE GEBIRGSJÄGER

Although the origins of *Gebirgsjäger* (mountain soldier) in the German army can be traced back only to comparatively recent times, the experiences of commanders reaching as far back as Alexander the Great and Hannibal the Carthaginian (and more recently Napoleon) in trying to negotiate mountainous regions presaged the need for specialist mountain soldiers.

Below: Tough men doing a tough job: an artillery mule team on a mountain path. The last mule carries wicker mats and tarpaulins for emplacing the gun.

Until such time as these were available, mountainous regions were considered by strategists to be at best hostile and at worst impassable, and certainly unsuitable terrain in which to conduct military operations. Large bodies of conventional troops were vulnerable in mountain areas, as evinced by the experience of British troops on the Northwest Frontier of India in the late nineteenth century. Here a numerically inferior force composed of small bands of Afghan tribesmen, highly mobile and with expert knowledge of the terrain, resisted a statistically superior force for a considerable time. As knowledge of the terrain and mobility were key to the success of the small-scale guerrilla actions against the British in northern India, so they were in the mountain battles of subsequent wars.

From the mid-nineteenth century, the introduction of railway networks across Europe vastly increased the speed at which an army could advance. This in turn gave cause for defence planners to turn their attentions to vulnerable mountain regions, and prompted the organisation of mountain troops in certain European armies. In Italy, Alpine troops were trained for operations along Italy's northern border; in France, which has mountains on its frontiers with Spain, Germany and Italy, the Chasseurs Alpins were raised; and Austro-Hungary, with mountainous borders with Italy to the south and Russia to the east, created the Schutzen. The close alliance between the Austro-Hungarian Empire and the newly unified Germany meant that responsibility for the defence of Germany's mountain regions fell to the Austro-Hungarian Army and, at least for a time, its Schutzen largely negated a need for a large German mountain army.

Although mountain training and equipment in the Reichswehr were not standardised until 1914, several formations existed in nineteenth-century Germany that can be regarded as the forerunners of the Gebirgsjäger. These were the Bavarian Jäger battalions, the Schlettstädter Jäger of the Vosges Mountains, the Goslarer Jäger in the Harz Mountains, and reaching further back, the Saxon sharpshooters recruited from among forestry officials in 1809.

Above: The building block of the Gebirgsjäger – a smiling private in service dress.

ALPENKORPS

On 20 October 1914, shortly after the outbreak of the First World War, the Royal Bavarian war ministry gave the order to build up a unit of soldiers on skis, and on 21 November the 1st Bavarian Schneeschuhbataillon was constituted in Munich. This first true German mountain unit was followed in December by the 2nd, 3rd and 4th Schneeschuhbataillons, and in Württemberg and in Prussia further Schneeschuh (snowshoe) units were raised. Half a year later these battalions had built the 3rd Jäger Regiment, which was attached to a newly formed German Alpenkorps.

The Alpenkorps drew men, mostly from the Württemberg and Bavarian armies, who were local to the mountains and, like their forebears, possessed the skills to conduct both offensive and defensive operations in this terrain. It was envisaged that they would also be employed as guides for the main body of the army, if compelled to pass over mountainous regions, or at times be called on to spearhead an assault. In general, however, there was a distinct shortage of men with Alpine knowledge in Germany, and mountaineering organisations were set up to create a pool of recruits with knowledge of rock climbing and survival skills.

In 1915, the Italian declaration of war against Austria triggered confrontations on the Alpine border between the two countries. With the need for skilled mountain troops now increasingly evident, the Alpenkorps was deployed from its base in Bavaria to Tirol in the Dolomites, on the southern part of the front. It was here that Erwin Rommel, then commander of a Württemburg Gebirgsjäger unit and later the legendary 'Desert Fox' of North Africa, won his 'Blue Max' (Pour le Mérite).

During the Great War, the Alpenkorps fought in Serbia in 1915 and in France at Verdun. In 1916 it was sent to the Romanian Carpathians. In 1917 it went to the Vosges, then again to Romania, and from there to the Alps for the Isonzo battles. In the final year of the war it fought in Flanders, at the River Somme and on the Bulgarian front. During the retreat through Hungary, it prevented the country's revolutionary regime from disarming it and reached German soil in good order.

Owing to the great success of the Alpenkorps in the First World War, the peacetime Reichswehr fought hard to retain its mountain troops. Despite the restriction to a 100,000 strong army imposed by the Versailles Treaty, several units were equipped with mountain gear and trained in mountain warfare in 1925, in the hope that these would form the basis of a future mountain fighting force. Recruits were at first drawn from the mountain-trained Bavarian State Police, and collectively these units were organised as the Gebirgs Brigade, the sole mountain unit at the time of the formation of the Wehrmacht in 1935. The brigade was initially commanded by Generalleutnant Ludwig Kübler and comprised the 98th, 99th and 100th Gebirgsjäger Regiments, in addition to the 79th Gebirgs Artillery Regiment. In August 1937 command of the brigade passed to General Hubert Lanz, and on 9 April 1938, it was formed into the 1st Gebirgs Division in Garmisch-Partenkirchen, Bavaria.

When mobilisation was ordered on 26 August 1939, the 1st Gebirgs Division had an establishment of three regiments, all based in and around Bad Reichenhall, while the four battalions of the 79th Gebirgs Artillery Regiment were located in the area of Garmisch-Partenkirchen. As the establishment of a Gebirgs division was two Jäger regiments, the 100th Regiment was deemed surplus to establishment, detached and, together with an artillery battalion from 79th Gebirgs Artillery Regiment, eventually formed the cadre of the 5th Gebirgs Division on 25 October 1940, in the Tirol region of Austria. The second regiment of the 5th Gebirgs was the former 85th Infantry Regiment, which became supernumerary when the 10th Infantry was upgraded to a Panzergrenadier division. The 10th Infantry also donated some of its artillery to the artillery regiment. Both Jäger regiments retained their original numbers, 85 and 100, although the artillery regiment was redesignated the 95th Gebirgs Artillery Regiment. Command was given to Generalmajor Julius Ringel, a veteran mountain soldier who had served in the First World War (and in the 3rd Austrian Mountain Division before this was amalgamated into the German Army, along with the rest of the Austrian Army, in 1938). The 5th Gebirgs Division was based in Salzburg, Austria, under *Wehrkreis* (war district) XVIII, although the personnel were predominantly from Bavaria.

READY FOR WAR

ROLE

The 5th Gebirgs Division was raised, trained and equipped in advance of the German campaign in Russia, in which it was envisaged that it would fight in its established role as mountain soldiers: that is, as specialist light infantry unburdened with equipment likely to impede rapid movement over difficult ground. Indeed, the terrain in which it was expected to operate dictated that the support elements available to traditional infantry divisions, such as heavy artillery, armoured vehicles or even tanks, more often than not were unavailable, even though in reality most of the battles in Russia were fought across lowland terrain. (Other 'mountain' divisions in fact spent so little time fighting in the mountains that the title seems somewhat inappropriate.) Although special weapons and vehicles were developed – lighter-calibre artillery and howitzers that could be disassembled and carried by pack mules, and lightweight cars – the Gebirgsjäger trained

Below: Mountain troops were expected to travel light, but adverse weather conditions, particularly at height, meant that they had to carry suitable clothing and equipment as well as their weapons. These soldiers are early in the war wearing greatcoats and comforters.

and fought principally as infantry assault formations.

In 1942 the German Army conducted exercises which demonstrated that standard infantry formations could operate successfully in the mountains, provided they were supported by specialist mountain troops. Although this seemed to obviate the need for the Gebirgsjäger, units continued to be raised until the end of the war. As a result of these exercises, between July 1942 and November 1943 some of the Gebirgstruppen, who had learned the skills of skiing and rock climbing from an early age, were creamed off to form specialist Hochgebirgs brigades. In total four battalions were raised, and it was intended that these would provide leadership for normal infantry regiments operating in mountainous terrain. Experience showed that there was no need for such units, and they were later stood down and absorbed into the standard Gebirgs divisions.

RECRUITING

Men for the 5th Gebirgs Division were recruited, at least initially, from the catchment area of Wehrkreis XVIII. This included the mountains of southern Bavaria, where an appreciation of Alpine terrain and the skills needed to fight and survive in it were instilled into young men from an early age. Later in the war, as manpower shortages began to bite, this and every other German division was forced to accept replacements of a lower calibre.

Above: Gebirgsjäger rifle section during training. Note that the section leader carries an MP38.

TRAINING

On arrival at the training depot, which for the Gebirgsjäger was at Garmisch-Partenkirchen in the shadow of the Zugspitz massif and the Waxenstein Mountain, the recruit was issued his equipment and assigned to his barracks. As was common practice in the German Army, whether he be a cook, truck driver, artilleryman or engineer, the recruit was required to train first and foremost in the skills of the infantry. Thus, Gebirgsjäger recruits had to endure basic training on the parade ground, in weapons drill and in other such standards of the military. As in most western armies (but unlike the Russians), the German soldier was trained and expected to be able to use any of the weapons he might come across and not just the one he was issued with. In times of need therefore the soldier could use rifle, heavy machinegun, the battalion mortars, battalion anti-tank guns or whatever weapon came to hand. Only after this training was completed were recruits allowed to specialise.

After about two weeks, the Oath of Allegiance was sworn. As with any other arm of the German army this was marked by a ceremony in which groups of six recruits would form a square on the parade ground and, with one hand on the Reich's War Flag (or in some cases a sword or a gun barrel draped with the regimental colours) and the other hand raised in a salute, would swear allegiance to God and country.

Later came more specialised instruction in rock climbing, cross-country skiing, compass marches, night marches and route marches. Great emphasis was placed on these as, not being part of a motorised formation, the Gebirgsjäger's main form of transportation was his own two feet.

The training syllabus was rooted in the knowledge that the mountain soldier in effect faces two dangers, the first being his enemy and the second his environment. Mountain areas can at times be inhospitable, subject to rapidly changing and hostile weather, rock slides and avalanches, often devoid of shelter, and unable to sustain the growth of plants and shrubs that would normally supplement the soldiers' rations. The troops were disciplined to conserve not just food but also ammunition, medical supplies and other material, as resupply would sometimes be difficult if not impossible. A serious wound could well result in death, as evacuation to a first aid post could take days, in some cases even weeks. Cover was often minimal. Whereas an infantryman on lower ground could dig a slit trench or dugout, mountain troops had no such a luxury. Rocks could sometimes be used to construct a 'sangar', like the ones that were used extensively during the battles for Monte Cassino, but the inside of these shelters could be lethal, with bullets and shells ricocheting around and splintering off razor-sharp lumps of rock.

Whenever Gebirgsjäger were employed, these and other hardships were commonplace. In Poland they undertook exhausting marches across vast plains. In Norway and Lapland they experienced the bitter Arctic weather; in the Balkans and Greece, the harsh and inhospitable mountains of Yugoslavia; the heat of the mountainous regions of Greece and Crete; and in Southern Russia the freezing conditions of the Caucasus Mountains. On many occasions they were involved in operations on normal terrain and proved themselves just as adept at fighting there. When used as conventional infantry, however, their specialist skills and training were wasted (a similar situation to that in which Fallschirmjäger troops found themselves), and the lack of fully motorised units within their divisional structure would often leave them at a disadvantage when employed in this role. The large volume of kit that they were expected to carry meant progress during an advance was slower than an equivalent motorised unit, and held many more dangers.

To cope with these demands, the Gebirgsjäger had above all to possess mental strength and physical stamina. These qualities were much in evidence among the ranks of the 5th Gebirgs Division and the best of the other mountain units, and a strong sense of camaraderie existed between them. During the later stages of the Second World War, men from other army formations were transferred to Gebirgs units to be trained as mountain troops but, although good soldiers, they could not develop the skills that seasoned Jäger had gained through years of experience from a very early age in their mountain towns and villages.

Above: Climbing – especially in Alpine conditions – is a skill that has to be learnt and practised assiduously. Early recruits came from Bavaria and many already possessed the basic climbing techniques that later recruits would need to learn.

ORGANISATION

The organisation of a Gebirgs Division followed the standard of the army. The division was composed of two Jäger regiments, each consisting of three Gebirgsjäger battalions and a headquarters group. In addition there was a regiment of artillery, and signals, engineer, semi-motorised reconnaissance, motorised anti-tank and medical units, as well as supply troops and administrative services.

The authorised strength of a typical mountain division was:

14,000 men
5,500–6,000 animals, including:
–   1,500 horses
–   4,300 pack animals
–   550 mountain horses
1,400 vehicles (including cars and motorcycles)
600 horse-drawn vehicles
13,000 rifles
2,200 pistols
500 machine pistols
416 light machine guns
66 light mortars

Below: The mountain troops were lucky with their commanders, such as the 'Hero of Narvik' General der Gebirgstruppen Eduard Dietl seen here during the operations in Norway.

44 medium mortars
75 anti-tank rifles
80 heavy machine guns
16 light infantry guns
24 light mountain guns
12 light mountain howitzers
12 heavy field howitzers
4 heavy infantry guns
39 anti-tank guns
12 light flak guns

Senior officers would often lead detachments that were usually no larger than battalion size (as this was realistically the largest force that could be deployed in mountain areas). The standard make-up of a battalion was 877 officers and men, organised into three Jäger companies, and usually one machine gun, one anti-tank and one heavy weapons company. Each Jäger company had an average complement of 147 men and was equipped with 12 machine guns, one anti-tank rifle and two 8 cm mortars (a little over 3 inches). Within the battalion, the German army had far fewer junior officers than other western armies (especially the Americans). This had the effect of encouraging senior NCOs and junior officers to assume more responsibility and thus show greater initiative than would be expected in other armies.

TACTICS

Above: A Gebirgsjäger company on a training march. The first five men are the MG08 machine gun crew carrying their weapon in sections.

Unique guidelines governed the operations and tactical deployment of the Gebirgstruppen. Underpinning these guidelines was the knowledge that preparation and planning are vital to mountain warfare, and this was constantly stressed in their fighting manuals. Meticulous preparation was required, no matter how small the operation being undertaken, for the omission of even the smallest item of kit, or an error in navigational could prove fatal.

As most mountainous areas at the time lacked adequate road networks, consideration had to be given to not only troop movements but also to movement of supply trains and the transportation of heavy equipment. Avalanches also proved a real and constant threat to these movements. Thus careful map reading and weather forecasting were vital to enable troops to avoid dangerous areas or pass through with minimal risk. To minimise the threat of avalanches when traversing a slope, men were carefully spaced in columns at 30-yard intervals, and zigzagged lightly as they moved. Once one group had made it to safe ground, the next group could then move off. Vertical ascents or descents were not allowed due to the risk of dislodging snow.

Later in the war, the 5th Gebirgs troops often found themselves, like Fallschirmjäger

Above: Another view of Dietl, here in the mountains with his staff officers. Note the usual variations in footware and puttees worn by mountain troops.

units, thrown into the line as ordinary infantry, far from their natural environment, and they frequently suffered as a result.

However, morale and esprit de corps in mountain troop units was almost universally very high, and commanders such as General der Gebirgstruppen Eduard Dietl, the 'Hero of Narvik', and 5th Gebirgs commander Julius 'Papa' Ringel were idolised by their men. When in their element – the high mountain peaks of Norway or the Caucasus – the Gebirgsjäger fought with an elan and determination that were second to none.

IN ACTION

On completion of training, the 5th Gebirgs Division was held in reserve at home for several months under XVIII Mountain Corps of the Second Army assigned to Army Group C. Then, in March 1941, it was posted to the Balkans to take part in the invasion of Greece: Operation 'Marita'. After the fall of Greece, it was landed on Crete, where it played a significant role in helping to secure the island from Allied forces that had been evacuated there. Following a spell of occupation duty on Crete, the division was posted back to Germany for rest and refitting. In March 1942, with the invasion of Russia already 10 months old, it was sent to the Eastern Front to take part in operations against Leningrad in the Volkhov region. Here it remained until November 1943, fulfilling the role of a 'fire brigade' for the Eighteenth Army, serving at various times on the Volkhov front, near Mga, near Schlüsselburg and on the Neva near Kolpino.

From the Eastern Front, the 5th Gebirgs Division was moved to Italy and in late 1943 arrived on the 'Gustav Line' near Cassino. It took part in the defensive battles up through Italy, encompassing actions on the Gustav Line at Cassino, and on the Gothic Line. Finally, late in the war, the division fought in the mountain region between France and Italy, before surrendering to US forces near Turin in May, 1945.

POLAND AND FRANCE

100th Gebirgsjäger Regiment, which was transferred in autumn 1940 to the newly constituted 5th Gebirgs Division, had been heavily involved in the Polish campaign. Fighting in the Carpathian Mountains, the regiment captured the important Dukla Pass. The following spring it was committed to the crossings of the Maas River and later the Loire. Although predating the formation of the 5th Gebirgs Division, these actions provided vital combat experience for the tough battles in Greece.

MUSSOLINI AND GREECE

In the autumn of 1940, as Hitler consolidated his control over much of northwest Europe, Italian forces launched a surprise invasion of Greece to help satisfy Mussolini's ambitions for a Mediterranean empire to rival the one that his ally was building in northern Europe. The attack, which came from occupied Albania on 28 October, soon bogged down in torrential rain and mud before the stalwart defence put up by the Greek armies. Counterattacks launched between November and the New Year soon had the Italian armies on the back foot.

Mussolini's actions had been intended to impress his ally, but in fact had the opposite effect. In private, a deeply angered Hitler referred to the invasion as a 'regrettable blunder', and his suspicions regarding the effectiveness of the Italian military increased. The attack had only succeeded in driving the Greeks into an closer alliance with the

Order of battle, 5th Gebirgsjäger Division, 1 January 1941

I./,II./,III./ 85th Gebirgsjäger Regiment

I./,II./,III./ 100th Gebirgsjäger Regiment

I./,II./,III./,IV./ 95th Gebirgs Artillery Regiment

95th Aufklärungs (Battalion) Reconnaissance Abteilung

95th Panzerjäger (Anti-tank) Abteilung (motorised)

95th Gebirgs Pionier (Engineer) Battalion

95th Nachrichten (Signals) Abteilung

95th Nachschubtruppen (supply troops)

Main units

85th Gebirgsjäger Regiment

100th Gebirgsjäger Regiment

100th Gebirgs Artillery Regiment

95th Radfahr Abteilung

95th Gebirgs Panzerjäger Abteilung

95th Gebirgs Pionier Abteilung

95th Gebirgs Nachrichten Abteilung

Above and Right: The first wholesale use of the Gebirgsjäger was during the Norway campaign when 3rd Gebirgsjäger under General Dietl performed to great effect. These two photographs of the campaign show: (above) the unit disembarking from a destroyer and (right) a signals section aboard a fishing boat at Narvik. Note the Edelweiss Gebirgsjäger badge on the right sleeve of the man at left. (See page 64 for more information on this.)

Left: DFS 230A glider carrying the 'combined operations' insignia for the Narvik campaign, incorporating a propeller for the Luftwaffe, an anchor for the Kriegsmarine and an Edelweiss for the Gebirgsjäger.

Below: Gebirgsjäger parade in Narvik after landing.

Above: Gebirgsjäger units made extensive use of animals – particularly pack animals – for artillery and transport. This supply column on the march is using some of the unit's authorised strength of 600 horse-drawn vehicles.

British, who honoured an earlier promise by landing troops on Crete and Lemnos, thus threatening Hitler's southern flank in advance of the invasion of Russia, and equally importantly, the vital Romanian oilfields. Hitler considered he had no choice but to send German forces to support the Italians, despite the setback to the timetable for the invasion of Russia, and ordered an invasion of Greece with a force of at least 10 divisions.

Operation 'Marita'

Planning for the invasion of Greece – Operation 'Marita' – at once began in earnest. This envisaged a limited move against eastern Thrace from Bulgaria, taking Salonika and the coast and pre-empting any attempt by the British to land behind the German advance into southern Russia. No further incursion was planned at this stage. However, these plans were upset by events in Yugoslavia where, in March 1941, a coup d'état against the pro-Axis regent installed a new government with an anti-German stance. Hitler now prepared another operation against Yugoslavia, codenamed '*Strafe*' (punishment), for the spring of 1941, to run concurrently with the attack on Greece. In the combined operation the Twelfth Army (Wilhelm List) was ordered to move on Greece, while the Second Army (M. F. von Weichs), Paul von Kleist's First Panzer Group and the Hungarian Third Army moved on Yugoslavia. The added burden actually produced a tactical advantage for the Greek operation. No longer would the German generals be restricted to a frontal assault on the formidable Metaxas Line along the Bulgarian–Greek frontier. They could now exploit the pathways into Greece that they had coveted from the start: the lightly defended passes leading from Yugoslavia.

For the operation the 5th Gebirgs Division was attached to XVIII Corps of the Twelfth Army, charged with penetrating the heavily defended 125-mile Metaxas Line that covered the Bulgarian border to the north and east of Salonika. In total, List's Twelfth Army numbered eight infantry divisions and the 2nd and 9th Panzer Divisions, divided among XL Panzer Corps (Georg Stumme), XVIII Mountain Corps (Franz Boehme), and XXX Corps (Otto Hartmann). They were faced by troops of the Greek Second Army (70,000 men) in the Metaxas Line, whose western flank was covered by the Yugoslav Fifth Army and the Greek 20th Infantry Division. To block an attempted thrust down the Aliakmon Valley west of Mount Olympus, the British had despatched an expeditionary force from North Africa under General Henry Maitland Wilson. This comprised some 75,000 men, including the 6th Australian Infantry Division, the 2nd New Zealand Division and the 1st Armoured Brigade, and could field some 100 tanks. The Australian 7th Division and a Polish brigade were intended for Greece as well, but were held back for North Africa, as Rommel was at that time advancing into Cyrenaica.

List's Operation 'Marita' is generally considered a masterpiece of military planning. Recognising the Yugoslav Fifth Army as the weak link in the Allied position, he struck out to the west at 05:15 on 6 April, before the Yugoslavs had time to complete mobilisation. As Weichs' Second Army thrust south into Yugoslavia from Austria, and Kleist's First Panzer Group pushed toward Belgrade from Bulgaria, Twelfth Army attacked Thrace, sending XL Corps westwards through the Vardar region toward Macedonia. On 7 April, the Kriva Pass and Skopje were taken after heavy fighting with the Yugoslav Third Army. But instead of heading for the Aliakmon Valley as the Allies anticipated, List then

ORDER OF BATTLE, 5th GEBIRGSJÄGER DIVISION, APRIL 1941

HQ
Staff Radio Support

95th Pionier Battalion
(Major Schatte)
1/95th Pionier Company
2/95th Pionier Company
3/95th Pionier Company

95th Panzerjäger Battalion
(Major Bindermann)
(37mm L/45 PAK 35/36)
1/95th PzJäg Company
2/95th PzJäg Company

95th Aufklärungs Battalion
(Major Graf Castell zu Castell)
1/95th Aufkl Company
2/95th Aufkl Company

95th Gebirgsjäger Artillery Regiment
(Oberstleutnant Wittmann)
I/95th Art Battalion, Major von Sternbach
(75mm L/19 GebG 36)
II/95th Art Battalion, Major Raithel
(105mm leFH)

85th Gebirgsjäger Regiment
(Oberst Krakau)
I. 85th Battalion Gebirgsjäger Regiment
(Major Dr Treck)
1st Gebirgsjäger Company
2nd Gebirgsjäger Company
3rd Gebirgsjäger Company
4th Gebirgsjäger Company
5th Gebirgsjäger Company

100th Gebirgsjäger Regiment
(Oberst Utz)
I/100th Gebirgsjäger Regiment
(Major Schrank)
1st Gebirgsjäger Company
2nd Gebirgsjäger Company
3rd Gebirgsjäger Company
4th Gebirgsjäger Company
5th Gebirgsjäger Company

II. Battalion/100th Gebirgsjäger
Regiment (Major Friedmann)
6th Gebirgsjäger Company
7th Gebirgsjäger Company
8th Gebirgsjäger Company
9th Gebirgsjäger Company
10th Gebirgsjäger Company

55th Krad (motorcycle recce) Battalion
1/55th Krad Company
2/55th Krad Company
4/55th Krad Company

84th Flak Battalion
(20mm L113 AA Flak 38)
1st Flak Company
2nd Flak Company
3rd Flak Company
4th Flak Company

Light Convoy 1
III/100th Gebirgsjäger Regiment
(Major Ehall)
(37mm L/45 PAK 35/36)
11th Gebirgsjäger Company
12th Gebirgsjäger Company
13th Gebirgsjäger Company
14th Gebirgsjäger Company
15th Gebirgsjäger Company

666 Pionier (Engineer) Battalion
1st Pionier Company
2nd Pionier Company
3rd Pionier Company
4th Pionier Company
3/7th Pionier

Light Convoy 2
II. 85th Battalion Gebirgsjäger Regiment
(Major Esch)
(37mm L45 PAK 35/36)
6th Gebirgsjäger Company
7th Gebirgsjäger Company
8th Gebirgsjäger Company
9th Gebirgsjäger Company
(75mm L/19 GebG 36)
10th Gebirgsjäger Company (MMG)

659th Pionier Battalion
1/659th Pionier Company
2/659th Pionier Company
3/659th Pionier Company
4/659th Pionier Company

I./118th Artillery Battalion
(105mm leFH)

85th Flak Battalion (20L113 AA
FLAK 38)
1st Flak Company
2nd Flak Company
3rd Flak Company
4th Flak Company
3/609th Motorised Flak (20L113 AA FLAK 38)

ordered XL Panzer Corps to attack through the strategically important Monastir Gap for Kozani, further west – the gateway into Greece on the open flank of the Allied line along the Vermion mountains and the Greek front in Albania.

The Metaxas Line

Meanwhile XXX Corps was moving on western Thrace and XVIII Mountain Corps preparing to assault the 'Metaxas' Line.

Beginning in April 1939, the Greek government had poured enormous sums of money into the construction of this system of defensive works in the mountains covering the Bulgarian border, which was named the Metaxas Line in honour of the then Prime Minister, Ioannis Metaxas. The defences consisted of heavily fortified concrete blockhouses, many of them interlinked by tunnels, and manned by first-rate Greek troops. In front of these were smaller outposts and weapons pits.

The German plan called for a frontal attack on this position, to be undertaken by one German infantry division and the reinforced 5th and 6th Gebirgs Divisions. In the days prior to the attack, the troops hauled ammunition and supplies from the Bulgarian town of Petrich up into their forward positions, sequestered on the wooded slopes below the enemy line. Observing the Gebirgsjäger at this task their comrades-in-arms began referring to them as the *Gamsbock* or 'mountain goats', a name that was enthusiastically adopted by the troops themselves. To support the infantry, artillery also had to be manhandled up the slopes.

By 05:00 on the morning of 6 April, the men of the 5th Gebirgs Division were poised for the attack. They had strapped rifles across their chests, and wire cutters, flare guns, entrenching tools and hand grenades hung from their belts. Shortly after 05:00 the gunners began to lay down a heavy preparation. Then flights of Ju87 Stukas approached to pound the ground positions, raising clouds of dust and grit that shrouded the mountaintops. While the bombs were still falling, the troops left the cover of the woods and scrambled up the snowy slopes that the Greeks had cleared of timber to provide their gunners with unrestricted fields of fire. Withering fire fell down on the advancing troops, proof that the large concrete and steel bunkers had largely withstood the barrage. Over the next few hours, in the face of extremely tough resistance from the Greek defenders, the mountain troops began to gouge holes in the line by clearing the trenches that flanked the bunkers. The engineers systematically blasted the casemates open with explosives or incinerated the defenders with flamethrowers aimed through the embrasures. Around midday the Greeks responded by calling in artillery fire on their own positions. Exposed on the slopes, the Gebirgsjäger huddled in the abandoned Greek trenches or burrowed into shell craters for protection. Through the afternoon and evening, the Greek troops emerged sporadically from their culverts in an effort to drive the Germans from the positions they had seized. But the men of the 5th Gebirgs Division were not about to give up their hard-won toeholds in the Metaxas Line. Bolstered

Below: Map showing the Metaxas Line and 5th Gebirgsjäger operations in the Balkans.

by reinforcements during the night, they attacked with renewed determination at dawn. Grappling up cliffs made slippery by the freezing rain, they blasted or burned the Greeks from one bunker after another.

Through the day, each carefully located nest of fortifications along the line of advance was gradually reduced through a combination of frontal and enveloping attacks, with tactical support from Luftwaffe aircraft. Using these methods the advanced units of the 5th Gebirgs Division, together with the reinforced 125th Infantry Regiment, finally penetrated the Metaxas Line on the evening of 7 April, pouring through large gaps in the line out onto the plain to the south. The savage contest cost the division 160 lives – nine more than the Wehrmacht had lost in the entire campaign in Yugoslavia.

Meanwhile the 6th Gebirgs Division crossed a 7,000-foot snow-covered mountain range and broke through the line at a point that had been considered inaccessible by the Greeks. The division reached the rail line to Salonika east of Lake Dojran on the evening of 7 April, and entered Kherson two days later.

After repelling several fierce counterattacks, the 5th Gebirgs Division moved on Neon Petritsi, and with this taken gained access to the important Rupul Gorge from the south. The 125th Infantry Regiment, which was attacking the gorge from the north, suffered such heavy casualties that it had to be withdrawn from further action after it had reached its objective.

Some of the fortresses in the line held out for days after the German attack divisions had bypassed them, and could not be reduced until heavy guns were brought up. However, in a deft move around the Metaxas Line, the 2nd Panzer Division motored west to the Yugoslav town of Strumica on 6 April, encountering little resistance on the way. The panzers then turned south towards the Greek border, brushed aside a Greek motorised infantry division near Lake Dojran, and took Salonika without a fight on 9 April. Coupled with the advance of XVIII Mountain Corps across the Metaxas Line, the armoured thrust succeeded in cutting off a large part of the Greek Second Army in Eastern Thrace and led to the collapse of Greek resistance east of the Vardar River. On 9 April the Greek Second Army surrendered unconditionally (the number of prisoners taken has never been established because the Germans released all Greek soldiers after disarming them). On the left wing, XXX Infantry Corps faced weaker opposition than west of the Nestos River, but had to overcome poor road conditions that delayed the movement of artillery and supplies. By the evening of 8 April, its attached 164th Infantry Division had captured Xanthi, while the 50th Infantry Division had advanced far beyond Komotini toward the Nestos, which both divisions reached on the next day.

Now only the newly formed Allied Group W, consisting of the British and Commonwealth forces and two inexperienced Greek divisions, stood in the way of the advance. In light of the capture of Salonika the group commander, Wilson, decided that a defence of Greece's northwest frontier was futile, and instead set up his main defensive line in a short arc extending westward from the Aegean coast near Mount Olympus to the Aliakmon River – a position that conceded northern Greece to the Germans but guarded the main approaches to Athens.

Stumme's XL Panzer Corps was even then poised at the northern end of the Monastir Gap, the strategic corridor from Yugoslavia to central Greece. On 10 April his lead units began to push through the narrows, and early the next morning ran into a 3,000-strong rearguard that Wilson had deployed on the panzer's route of advance in anticipation of the onslaught. Although eventually forced to withdraw, they succeeded in delaying the German advance, giving Wilson valuable time to establish his main line.

The rapid advance of XL Panzer Corps was now seriously jeopardising the position of the Greek First Army in Albania. However, it was not until 13 April that the first Greek elements began to pull back toward the Pindus Mountains. On the same day Stumme

Above: Mountain bivouac.

Above: General Ringel (second right) and a senior staff officer meet sympathetic fighters in Yugoslavia.

ordered the Leibstandarte Division and 73rd Infantry Division to the crossroads at Kastoria to stop the stream of retreating Greek troops, and the following 48 hours witnessed heavy fighting. On 19 April the 1st SS Regiment was ordered to advance southeastward in the direction of Yanina, to cut off the Greeks' route of withdrawal to the south and complete their encirclement. Realising the hopelessness of the situation, the Greek commander offered to surrender his 14 divisions. After brief negotiations, the surrender was accepted with honourable terms for the defeated. In recognition of the valour with which the Greek troops had fought, their officers were permitted to retain their side arms. The soldiers were not treated as prisoners of war and were allowed to go home after the demobilisation of their units.

Mount Olympus

As the advance continued apace, Boehme, XVIII Mountain Corps commander, had been forced to wait until the rear elements of his divisions that were lagging behind in the Rhodope Mountains were able to close up. The advance in the direction of the Vardar River was resumed as soon as the bulk of the corps had been reassembled. Once the Vardar crossing had been accomplished on 11 April, 6th Gebirgs Division drove in the direction of Edhessa and then turned southward toward Verroia. After capturing that town the division established a bridgehead across the Aliakmon and pushed on to the high ground at the foothills of Mount Olympus. The 2nd Panzer Division, with the 5th Gebirgs and 72nd Infantry Divisions closing up along the route of advance, continued on the left flank down the Aegean coast. The force crossed the Aliakmon near the river bend and entered Katerini on 14 April. That same day, the lead units reached a point where the slopes of Mount Olympus drop sharply to the sea.

Meanwhile the remainder of Stumme's force continued the advance in the direction of Athens and the Allied line. On 13 April, the 9th Panzer Division clashed with a British tank brigade at Ptolemais, devastating Wilson's armoured reserves. That same evening the division established a bridgehead across the Aliakmon River, and on the next day captured Kozani on the west side of the Vermion Mountains. For the next three days, however, the advance was stalled in front of the strongly fortified mountain positions held by the British.

Now without armoured support, Wilson reached the conclusion that his position was no longer tenable. The rapid progress of XL Panzer Corps was alarming enough, but in recent days General Boehme's XVIII Mountain Corps had regrouped in Salonika and was advancing down the Aegean coast.

With the threat of encirclement by these two pincers looming, and reinforcement from elsewhere in the Mediterranean out of the question, Wilson reluctantly ordered a withdrawal from the Vermion Mountains and lower Aliakmon River to Thermopylae, leaving rearguard units to hold up the advance.

Simultaneously with the main thrust into central Greece, the Twelfth Army completed the pacification of eastern Macedonia, western Thrace and the Aegean Islands. Following its capitulation, the Greek Second Army was demobilising in orderly fashion, leaving only isolated hostile forces active in these areas. Airborne units, together with elements of the 6th Gebirgs Division, were employed in the seizure of some of the larger Cyclades and Sporadhes Islands.

On the coast 2nd Panzer worked through an attack on rearguard positions held by New Zealand XXI Battalion on the Platomon Ridge. At first the tanks tried a frontal assault but made no headway. Then an infantry battalion managed to climb the western side of the ridge and encircle the defenders, who were forced to retreat to the Pinios Gorge, the last potential stronghold before Thermopylae.

Here the New Zealanders were reinforced by two Australian battalions and some artillery, which thwarted initial attempts by the panzers to push through the gorge at dawn on 18 April. However, hoping to outflank the New Zealand battalion, Boehme had dispatched the 6th Gebirgs Division on an arduous trek across the mountains to seal the western exit of the gorge. In the afternoon, infantry began to cross the Pinios River on floats, secured the road on the far side, and effectively cut off the defenders' line of retreat. Lacking proper radio equipment and fighting in isolated units, the defenders did not realise their plight and were all but annihilated in the ensuing struggle. With the fighting for the Pinios Gorge at an end, XVIII Mountain Corps entered the Plain of Thessaly hard on the heels of the Allied forces. The two days that it had taken for Boehme's corps to break through had been just sufficient for Wilson to pull back his right wing and avoid encirclement.

Larisa

During the night of 17 April, the rapid advance of XVIII Mountain Corps onto the Plain of Thessaly, threatening the British route of withdrawal through Larisa, forced an evacuation of the Aliakmon position. The British succeeded in breaking contact with the German outposts and left their positions, which had remained intact throughout the relentless attacks. On 19 April, the first XVIII Mountain Corps troops entered the town, where they found extensive stocks that the British had not had time to destroy. The capture of Larisa also brought the prize of the airfield, where the British had left their supply dumps intact.

During the fighting in the Mount Olympus area, the corps had encountered severe logistical problems because of the bad roads and traffic congestion. These difficulties had been only partially alleviated by airdrops and by shipping ammunition, rations and gasoline by lighter along the Aegean coast. The capture of rations and fuel stocks at

Below: Mountain infantry company on the march.

Larisa, ensured that Boehme's spearhead units were able to leave the Lamia area with adequate supplies. At Volos too, the Germans captured large quantities of diesel and crude oil, although Volos, the only port in central Greece that had a satisfactory capacity, could not be cleared of mines before 27 April.

For the German forces it was now primarily a question of maintaining contact with the retreating British forces and countering their evacuation plans. The infantry divisions were withdrawn from action because they lacked mobility. The 2nd and 5th Panzer Divisions, the 1st SS Motorised Infantry Regiment, and the 5th and 6th Gebirgs Divisions were ordered to continued the pursuit. As early as 16 April, the German command had realised that the British were evacuating their troops aboard ships at Volos and Piraeus. Numerous units were re-embarked during the last few days before the ports fell on 21 April.

XL Panzer Corps drive

Simultaneously with Boehme's advance down the Aegean coast, the 9th Panzer Division was attacking the western Aliakmon positions. In the face of stout defence by New Zealand troops, Stumme sent the bulk of his force on a wide flanking movement beyond the fringe of the British line, but this could only move at a crawl on appalling roads and took until 17 April to arrive. As soon as General Stumme realised that the enemy rearguard had withdrawn beyond the immediate reach of his spearheads, he issued orders giving Luftwaffe ground personnel traffic priority along the Kozani–Larisa road, as large-scale demolitions were delaying the German pursuit on the ground. However,

Below: Mountain troops on the Balkans Front make use of an 'acquired' Italian Semovente L40 da 47/32 SP gun. Armoured vehicles were not part of the Gebirgsjäger establishment, officially at least.

tactical air support units were able to operate from fields close to the fast-moving mobile forces, and harried the retreating British columns incessantly.

Thermopylae Pass

It appeared to all eyes that the not so distant calamity at Dunkirk was about to be repeated in the Balkans. Mindful of this General Wilson ordered a rearguard to make a last stand at Thermopylae Pass, the gateway to Athens, to permit the evacuation of the main body of British forces. On the evening of 21 April German air reconnaissance information indicated that the British defence line consisted of light field fortifications, the construction of which did not seem to have progressed beyond the initial stage. Other air reconnaissance reports showed that British troops were still being evacuated from the ports of Piraeus and Khalkis.

By 22 April a flying column of the 5th Panzer Division was attacking the Thermopylae positions defended by ANZAC infantry, artillery and armour. Although the initial German probing attacks were unsuccessful, a wide enveloping movement was undertaken the next day by 6th Gebirgs Division troops who crossed the difficult terrain west of the ANZAC positions. This operation took place in concert with another outflanking manoeuvre performed by a tank-supported motorcycle battalion advancing via Molos. After offering strong resistance along the Molos road, the ANZAC troops abandoned the Thermopylae Pass during the night of 24–25 April.

Drive on Athens

After abandoning the Thermopylae area the British rearguards withdrew to an improvised position south of Thebes, where they erected a last obstacle in front of Athens. The motorcycle battalion of the 2nd Panzer Division, which had crossed to the island of Euboea to seize the port of Khalkis and had subsequently returned to the mainland, was given the mission of outflanking the British rearguard. The motorcycle troops encountered only slight resistance, and on the morning of 27 April the first Germans entered the Greek capital. They captured intact large quantities of fuel, several thousand tons of ammunition, 10 trucks loaded with sugar and 10 truckloads of other rations in addition to various other equipment, weapons and medical supplies.

By 30 April the last British troops had either escaped or been taken prisoner and hostilities ceased. During the spectacular campaign in Greece, List captured 90,000 Yugoslavs, an estimated 270,000 Greeks, and more than 12,000 British, Australian and New Zealand troops. However, although the BEF lost much of its vital heavy equipment during the Greek campaign, some 50,000 men were able to make good their escape to the island of Crete.

List's own losses were 1,100 killed and 4,000 wounded or missing. After the fall of Athens the Twelfth Army and 5th Gebirgs Division stayed in Athens, where they enjoyed a brief rest before the next phase of the Balkans conquest got underway.

Below: The ability to move quickly over rough terrain without heavy equipment made demands on the skill and ingenuity of the Gebirgs engineers.

Above: Map of Crete.

CRETE

Recognising the supremacy of the Royal Navy in the Eastern Mediterranean, Hitler intended to break off the Balkans campaign in southern Greece. But the rout of Allied forces in Greece left them badly weakened, and Luftwaffe commanders were quick to recognise the opportunity to seize another prize – the island of Crete – by airborne assault.

The strategic importance of Crete lies in its position guarding access to the Eastern entrances to the Mediterranean, and during the Second World War it also offered an important staging point for flights to North Africa. British forces had occupied the island in October 1940 with a view to using it for future operations in the Balkans, the source of much of Germany's oil and minerals. Furthermore, the occupation offered an opportunity to maintain naval supremacy in the eastern Mediterranean, as the Cretan port of Suda provided the Mediterranean Fleet with a forward base 420 miles north of Alexandria.

The staff of Luftflotte 4 – which had been committed to the Balkans under command of Alexander Löhr – conceived the idea of capturing the island with airborne forces and forwarded the plan to Göring at the time of the invasion of Greece. He thought highly of it but the OKW (Oberkommando der Wehrmacht) preferred action against Malta, a crucial link in the Allied chain of supply to North Africa.

However, on 20 April, after a conference with Generalleutnant Kurt Student (commander of XI Fliegerkorps), Hitler decided in favour of Crete. His decision was influenced by two key factors. First, any opportunity to remove the threat to the Ploesti oilfields in Romania warranted attention. As an added incentive, capture of the island would offer an ideal forward base from which to conduct offensive air and naval operations and

to support the ground offensive in Egypt. Hitler was adamant that there was to be no further delay to the start of the Russian campaign, and five days later Directive No. 28 (Operation 'Merkur' – Mercury) was issued. This was to be a Luftwaffe operation under the executive responsibility of General Löhr, and was scheduled for 16 May.

Although both Luftflotte 4 and XI Fliegerkorps submitted detail plans, it was the latter's scheme that was adopted. Since the troops were to be entirely resupplied by air in the initial stages, success depended on the capture of one of Crete's airfields. Recognising this fact, the XI Fliegerkorps plan envisaged the simultaneous landing of gliders and air drop of parachute troops at seven points. The first wave of airborne troops was to strike at H-Hour against Maleme and Canea. The second wave was to descend at H plus 8 hours on Rethymnon (modern Retimo) and at Heraklion. These 15,000 combat troops were to link up from distances of about 10 to 80 miles apart as soon as possible.

On the second day, elements of the 5th Gebirgs with heavier weapons were to be airlifted to the three airfields captured by the first assault, followed by a third wave carried across the sea to Heraklion, Suda Bay and any minor ports open to shipping in Konteradmiral Karlgeorg Schüster's convoy. This would land 6,000 further troops and heavy equipment that could not be airlifted, including the field guns, anti-tank guns and panzers of the 31st Panzer Regiment, ammunition, rations and other supplies. The Royal Navy maintained a strong naval presence around Crete, and there were no Kriegsmarine units available. The convoys were made up largely of small caiques and coastal freighters that had been captured during the Greek campaign and were assembled in the port of Piraeus. Clearly, the convoys would be frighteningly vulnerable if still at sea at night, when the Luftwaffe could not provide air cover and the Royal Navy ruled the sea.

Throughout the operation, the 716 fighters, bombers and recce aircraft of VIII Fliegerkorps would be providing powerful tactical support. This was the formation which

Above: 5th Gebirgsjäger Division was the follow-up force during Operation 'Merkur' on Crete. A significant number of men was to be air-landed. Here, members of the division wait next to the Junkers Ju52 transports.

Above: Many mountain troops were transported by sea during the battles for Greece and Crete. Loaded at Piraeus and Chalkis in flotillas of Greek caiques, two battalions of the 85th Gebirgsjäger Regiment were en route to Crete with an escort of Italian warships when the Royal Navy intercepted the convoy. Over 500 Gebirgsjäger died in the battle.

had swept the Royal Air Force out of Greece in April and achieved almost total domination of the skies over Crete in the first weeks of May.

Considered in hindsight, this plan had the advantage of putting the Germans in possession of all strategic points on the island in one lightning strike, after which a follow-up operation would clear any remaining pockets of opposition. But dispersing the troops over great areas, inevitably without tactical air support at certain junctures, was a boldly calculated risk. Furthermore, from the outset of the operation, the absence of the airborne troops of the VIII Fliegerkorps Infantry Division was to be a major problem. It could not be transferred in time for the operation from Romania, where it guarded the Ploesti oil fields, and the 5th Gebirgs Division, which was brought in to replace it, had no practical experience in airborne operations.

All units for Operation 'Merkur' were hurriedly assembled within two weeks, although logistical problems caused the start date to be put back to 20 May. Student's XI Fliegerkorps was to be responsible for the actual assault on the island. It had 10 air transport wings with a total of approximately 500 Ju52 transports and 80 DFS 230 gliders available to airlift the attacking forces from recently captured airfields in Greece. The assault troops consisted of the *Luftlande Sturmregiment* (Air-landed Assault Regiment – Generalmajor Eugen Meindl), the 7th Flieger Division (Generalleutnant Wilhelm Süssmann) and the 5th Gebirgs Division under Ringel.

The topography of Crete in many ways favoured the invader, because at that time there were virtually no communication lines running north–south down the 160-mile-long, narrow, barren island. The only usable port on the south coast was the small harbour of Sphakia, which was inaccessible to motor traffic. In the north the only efficient port was in Suda Bay, connected by a single road that ran close to the north coast with the towns of Maleme, Canea, Rethymnon and Heraklion. The British defenders, who could only resupply Crete from Egypt, were handicapped by the shortage of adequate ports, and by the fact that their airfields were situated close to the exposed north coast at Maleme, Rethymnon and Heraklion.

At the beginning of the German invasion of Crete, the swollen island garrison consisted of about 27,500 British and Imperial troops and 14,000 Greeks under the command of Major-General Bernard C. Freyberg, commander of the New Zealand division. The original garrison, numbering approximately 5,000 men, was fully equipped, but the troops evacuated from Greece were battle weary, disorganised, and equipped only with the small arms they had saved during the withdrawal. Furthermore, the Greek and Cretan soldiers were mostly inadequately armed recruits. There was a general shortage of heavy equipment, transportation and supplies. The armour available to the defenders consisted of eight medium, and 16 light tanks, and a few personnel carriers; these were divided equally among the four groups formed in the vicinity of the airfields and near Canea. The artillery was composed of some captured Italian guns with a limited supply of ammunition, ten 3.7-inch howitzers and a few anti-aircraft batteries. The construction of fortifications was far behind schedule.

During May 1941 the British air strength on Crete never exceeded 36 planes, and only half of these were operational at any time. With the German preparatory attacks from the air growing

Above: 'O group' on Crete.

in intensity and the British unable to operate from their airfields, the latter decided to withdraw their last few planes the day before the invasion began. Thus, all told, Crete was ill equipped to face an attack from the air. Freyberg, however, regarded such an operation as impractical and dispersed his ground forces with a view to preventing seaborne landings in Suda Bay and the adjacent beaches, and airborne landings on the three airfields at Maleme, Rethymnon and Heraklion. He divided his forces into four self-supporting groups, the strongest of which was assigned to the defence of the vital Maleme airfield. The lack of transportation made it impossible to organise a mobile reserve force.

The British naval forces defending Crete were based on Suda Bay, where the port installations were under constant attack during the period immediately preceding the invasion, restricting the unloading of supplies to the early hours of the morning. The only aircraft carrier in the eastern Mediterranean was unable to provide fighter cover because of aircraft losses during the evacuation of Greece.

The British were well appraised from their Ultra intelligence intercepts of the German intentions against Crete, and their counter-measures were based on the assumption that an airborne invasion could not succeed without the landing of heavy weapons, reinforcements and supplies by sea. By intercepting these at sea, Freyberg believed, 'Crete will be held'.

At 07:15 on the morning of 20 May, after a short, vicious pounding from the air had driven the defenders into their bunkers, I Battalion of the Luftlande Sturmregiment began landing their DFS 230 gliders at Maleme Airfield, where they immediately ran into heavy opposition from the XXII New Zealand Battalion on Hill 107, and the 5th New Zealand Brigade.

Meanwhile, a gliderborne assault by Kampfgruppe Altmann (1 and 2 Companies of the Luftlande Sturmregiment) was heading to secure vital objectives near Canea, to split the main force of defenders. But as Hauptmann Altmann's men tried to land on the Akrotiri Peninsula near the AA emplacements, a storm of flak was roused that destroyed four gliders and scattered the rest. Once on the ground, Altmann discovered that the emplacement was a dummy, and within hours his No 2 Company had ceased to exist. No 1 Company under Oberleutnant Genz landed in nine gliders southeast of Canea and captured the AA batteries, but had to then withdraw southwards to join the other paratroops who had dropped there, as they were unable to link up with Altmann.

Above: The Kübelwagen was the largest vehicle that could fit inside a Ju52 troop carrier and was much used by motorised units of mountain regiments, such as the anti-tank companies.

Chaos still ruled on the ground as the first wave of paratroops roared over the coast, heading for Maleme. Groundfire brought down several Ju52s, but the drop of II and IV Battalions onto positions west of the airfield, and of III Battalion to the east, began as planned. II and IV Battalions landed virtually unopposed but III Battalion came down over strong Allied positions. Of the 600 men who jumped, 400 were killed – many before they reached the ground.

Meanwhile, a German force consisting of I, II and III Battalions of the 3rd Fallschirmjäger Regiment and an engineer battalion was dropped near Canea. III Battalion parachuted directly onto positions held by the 10th New Zealand Brigade and sustained heavy casualties. So too did the engineer battalion, which dropped to the southwest onto the fury of a Greek regiment. When the fighting abated, the commander of the regiment gathered together the survivors: scarcely 1,000 of his original 3,000 men. The combined efforts of I and II Battalions succeeded in securing Agia, but during the day the regiment was unable to progress in the direction of Canea and the situation appeared critical.

By midday on 20 May, none of the prime objectives assigned to the first wave had been secured. The Luftlande Sturmregiment had failed to take Hill 107 and Maleme airfield, and the 3rd Fallschirmjäger Regiment was hemmed in around Agia in what was termed 'Prison Valley'. Communications with headquarters on the Greek mainland had been practically non-existent. Furthermore, problems with refuelling the Ju52s and the dust on the Greek airfields were disrupting the timetable for the second wave.

Because of these logistical problems the second wave could only be dropped piecemeal, instead of en masse as planned. At 15:00 I and III Battalions of the 2nd Fallschirmjäger Regiment began landing at Rethymnon, in a sector held by elements of the 19th Australian Brigade. Many were scattered and some troops were dropped in the wrong place, with many injured when landing on rocky ground. However, the few hundred survivors managed to drive the Australians from a hill and set up a roadblock to prevent Allied reinforcements from moving in.

The final drop, three battalions of paratroops totalling 2,000 men, was to capture Heraklion, the ancient capital of the island. This drop descended into carnage when Australian AA gunners unleashed a torrent of fire on the transports as they lumbered overhead. Fifteen were lost, and troops from the surviving aircraft were widely dispersed in a chaotic drop that lasted for nearly three hours. In the face of such a determined defence there appeared little chance of taking the airfield at Heraklion that day.

The operation was now perilously close to crisis. On the first day Student had lost thousands of his elite troops, nearly a third of the 7th Division. Gruppe West had managed to gain a foothold at Maleme but had not taken the hill or the airfield, Gruppe Mitte was in a critical situation at Canea and Rethymnon, and Gruppe Ost had failed to gain Heraklion or the airfield there. News was then received that the flotilla of boats carrying the 5th Gebirgs Division reinforcements to Heraklion had been delayed and would not be ready to depart until the next day.

At this critical juncture, Student decided that the foothold on the western edge of the airfield and northwest shoulder of Hill 107 at Maleme was the one position that could be exploited. He decided to concentrate on Maleme and employ the 5th Gebirgs Division there instead of in the Heraklion sector. The new plan was to roll up the British and Dominion positions from the west, despite the risk of a counterattack by Freyberg.

Maleme

Early on 21 May, a stroke of fortune befell the Germans. Convinced that he was about to be overrun, the commander of XXII New Zealand Infantry Battalion made the crucial mistake of ordering back A and B Companies from Hill 107, overlooking Maleme airfield. In the confusion, small parties of German paratroops moved cautiously up the hill and found it abandoned. Student seized the moment to take his gamble. At 05.00, with the airfield still under artillery fire, the first Ju52s came in at wave-top level for a straight-in landing run at Maleme, carrying a full battalion and the headquarters staff of the 100th Gebirgsjäger Regiment. With shells exploding around the landing aircraft the scene rapidly became chaotic, with burning machines wrecked in collisions or by artillery fire littering the field.

By evening the bulk of the battalion was on the ground and had reinforced the Maleme sector. A further air drop of the reserves of the 1st and 2nd Fallschirmjäger Regiments in the early afternoon finally overran the airfield defences, and it seemed that Student now held the key to victory.

The situation remained serious, however. There were still fewer than 1,800 Germans fit for action; the Allies had 7,000 troops, and another 6,000 within 10 miles. Gruppe Mitte near Rethymnon and Gruppe Ost near Heraklion faced heavy concentrations of Allied troops. To the west of the airfield Hauptmann Wiedemann's III Battalion had to dig in near Perivolia just east of the town. The Germans managed to hold out for several days against determined counterattacks by heavy artillery and armour.

Convoy disaster

Since there were not enough aircraft to carry out both the initial landing and the rapid build up of forces on the island, a flotilla of 63 requisitioned Greek vessels had been put together in advance of the attack to carry part of the 5th Gebirgs Division to the island. Most of these commandeered vessels were caiques – a type of fishing boat dependent on a sail and a small auxiliary engine – and the rest of them a motley mix of coastal freighters. There were to be two flotillas; one was to carry some 2,300 Gebirgsjäger to Maleme; the other to carry 4,000 to Heraklion. On the night of 19 May, the first flotilla arrived at the island of Milos and anchored there. But with the situation on Crete grown critical, a change of plan occurred and both convoys were ordered to sail to Maleme. The first convoy departed on 20 May escorted by one small Italian corvette. At around 22:00, making only 7 knots, and still some 18 miles from the landing beaches at Maleme, they

Below: Piraeus harbour – Gebirgsjäger talk with the Italian sailors who would form their escort.

Above: A Cretan donkey pressed into service.

were picked out by the probing searchlights of a British naval task force led by Admiral Rawlings. Unknown to the ships crews, they had been spotted that afternoon by a British reconnaissance aircraft. For two and a half hours the British hunted the caiques and freighters down, sinking 12 of them. The survivors straggled back north towards Greece, leaving many of the Gebirgsjäger floating in their lifejackets in the warm waters. The III Battalion of the 100th Gebirgsjäger Regiment was decimated by the naval action and virtually disappeared as a fighting force. In the morning, Italian boats and planes mounted a rescue effort, and as the Ju52s resumed the airlift of the 100th Gebirgsjäger Regiment into Maleme, the troops in the planes dropped life-rafts to their comrades below. Some 178 survivors were rescued by seaplanes and another 64 by launches. By 16:00 in the afternoon on 22 May, the rescue effort had been completed, and miraculously only 300 of the 2,331 on board the ill-fated flotilla were dead. A few managed to reach land, suffering from exposure but still carrying their weapons!

The second flotilla set sail southwards from Milos on 22 May. At about 09:30 they came within range of another naval task force under Admiral King, but were saved by the timely arrival of Luftwaffe aircraft that forced King to break off the attack. This second flotilla was recalled to spare it the same fate as the first, and no further seaborne landings were attempted until the island was in German control.

22 May saw renewed action by the Luftwaffe against the British naval task forces in which two cruisers and a destroyer were sunk, and two battleships and two cruisers damaged. After these attacks, Admiral Cunningham, commander of the Mediterranean fleet, decided that he could not risk further losses by operating during the day near Crete or in the Aegean Sea, and withdrew.

Reinforcements and supplies were now arriving on Crete in a steady stream. By midnight on 22 May, the whole of I Battalion of the 100th Gebirgsjäger Regiment had been brought in, followed by II Battalion, I Battalion of the 85th Gebirgsjäger Regiment and then the 95th Gebirgs Engineer Battalion under Major Schatte. That evening the 5th Gebirgs Division's commander, Generalmajor Julius Ringel, flew in with orders to clear the British out of Crete. He assumed command of all forces in the Maleme area, and set about organising the forces there into three *Kampfgruppen* (battle groups). Kampfgruppe Schatte was to protect the Maleme area from any western threat and push westwards to capture Kastelli. A second group, made up of paratroops under command of Oberst Ramcke, was to strike northwards to the sea to protect the airfield and then extend eastwards along the coast. The third, under the command of Oberst Utz, was to move eastwards into the mainland, in a flanking movement across the mountains. The New

Zealand commanders had already opted to withdraw to strengthened positions in readiness for the German advance, but in effect, as Freyberg's chief of staff later remarked, 'this amounted to accepting the loss of Crete'.

Above: General Ringel with staff officers questions captured British troops on Crete.

On 23 May, the three battle groups moved cautiously forward. I Battalion of the 85th Gebirgsjäger Regiment headed eastwards of Kampfgruppe Utz and reached the village of Modi in the afternoon, where it was engaged by New Zealand troops. To outflank the enemy position, I Battalion of the 100th Gebirgsjäger Regiment marched across the mountains to the south, and after a brisk fire fight the village fell. Next, advancing up the bare slope of a tactically important position known as Hill 259, the Gebirgsjäger fought hand-to-hand with the New Zealand defenders. During the night they pulled back to avoid being cut off, and moved their artillery back southeast of Platanias. As a result of these actions, Maleme airfield was left virtually undefended.

On each line of advance, the German troops were harried incessantly by Greek and Cretan irregulars. Numerous reports were already circulating that these bands had carried out atrocities on the German dead and wounded – some of whom were apparently tortured before dying. Then, on the west of the island, the 95th Engineer Battalion came under attack from armed civilians (including women and children), and as a result the 5th Gebirgs Division announced that henceforth, for every German soldier killed in this fashion, 10 Cretans would be shot in reprisal. The Luftwaffe also dropped leaflets warning the population of the measures that would be taken against partisan activity.

With the pressure on Maleme eased, the volume of traffic into the airfield increased dramatically, to about 20 aircraft every hour. II Battalion of the 100th Gebirgsjäger Regiment, newly landed in the morning, was sent eastwards to support Kampfgruppe

Top and Above: Two members of a Gebirgsjäger mortar team. The man at top carries a rangefinder, the one below the mortar.

Utz. As more and more reinforcements landed on the island Ringel was able to regroup. During the night of 24–25 May, the 100th Gebirgsjäger Regiment gained contact with the paratroops under Oberst Heidrich, who had been surrounded in 'Prison Valley' since the 20th.

During the day, the 95th Gebirgs Engineer Battalion entered Kastelli to the west after air support from Stukas. Meanwhile, southwest of Canea, Oberst Ramcke's paratroops continued the advance from Pirgos along the coastline on the left flank. In the centre Kampfgruppe Utz, with two battalions of the 100th Gebirgsjäger Regiment, ran into the 10th New Zealand Brigade at Galatas. Fierce hand-to-hand combat raged between the mountain troops and the New Zealanders in the afternoon heat, but by nightfall two Gebirgs battalions had succeeded in forcing their way into the village. As they edged along the narrow streets in the dark, a counterattack by two companies of XXIII Battalion and the 5th New Zealand Brigade, supported by two tanks, forced Utz to retreat back into the surrounding hills, but the defenders were withdrawn to Canea on Freyberg's orders during the night and the next morning the mountain troops were able to re-enter the village.

Early in the morning of 27 May, Ringel began to attack Canea in earnest, as he deployed a battle group of two battalions of the 141st Gebirgsjäger Regiment (which had arrived on the 25th and 26th) under command of Oberst Jais on the right of the 100th Gebirgsjäger Regiment.

In front of Canea the British had deployed a rearguard dubbed 'Force Reserve'. It resisted fiercely, but of its 1,200 soldiers only 400 were able to escape the encircling Germans. By 15:00 on the 27th, the 100th Gebirgsjäger Regiment had penetrated the town defences.

Late in the evening before Canea fell, and despite suggestions that he retreat to Rethymnon, Freyberg ordered a general withdrawal through the mountains to the fishing village of Sphakia, where the ships of the Royal Navy were waiting to evacuate his forces. To the southwest of Suda, the 141st Gebirgsjäger Regiment beat back counterattacks by New Zealand and Australian troops. Unbeknown to Ringel, this was actually a rearguard action aimed at slowing his advance. When the Germans finally entered Canea and Suda bay, they found the area deserted.

Relief at Rethymnon

Oberstleutnant Wittmann's 95th Gebirgs Artillery Regiment was now ordered by Ringel to advance east as quickly as possible toward Rethymnon, and then Heraklion, to relieve the paratroopers cut off there. Under pressure from Student, who was agonising over the fate of his men, Ringel seconded virtually every mobile unit to Wittmann's command. Early on 28 May, Kampfgruppe Wittmann began the advance along the coast via Suda, where the road was found to be blocked by craters blown by a British commando unit that had landed during the night. A flanking attack was mounted, while mortars, anti-tank and mountain guns opened against New Zealand Maori troops and commandos behind the obstacle. At midday, resistance was overcome and contact with elements of Kampfgruppe Krakau was gained. From here the pursuit continued without interference as far as Kaina, where Kampfgruppe Wittmann met up with the main force. Lacking good observation points for artillery, Wittmann had to wait for support from Kampfgruppe Krakau, but by last light the odds were turned.

The pursuit continued on the 29th; Rethymnon was entered at 13:00 and contact with III Battalion of the 2nd Fallschirmjäger Regiment established. After a further artillery bombardment, the 700 Allied defenders, short of almost all supplies and unaware of the evacuation order of 27 May, laid down their arms. They had inflicted terrible losses on the 2nd Fallschirmjägers: 700 dead and wounded, 500 captured. Fewer than 200 men from the once proud regiment were still fit to fight when relief arrived.

Although the evacuation order had not reached Allied troops in Rethymnon, it had been received at Heraklion. Leaving the wounded behind, 4,000 men were embarked during the night of 28–29 May aboard ships under the command of Admiral Rawlings.

Leaving a detachment to guard the prisoners at Rethymnon, Kampfgruppe Wittmann resumed the march east toward Heraklion at 07:30 on the 30th. An hour later contact was made with the eastern group of the 2nd Fallschirmjäger Regiment. At 11:45 contact was gained with a reconnaissance patrol from the 1st Fallschirmjäger Regiment, which had been holding out in the Heraklion area since the afternoon of the first day. The advance continued with a couple of tanks (which had been landed by sea) leading the way for safety. The airfield and town were taken without a shot being fired.

Sphakia

Wittmann's drive to rescue the paratroops at Rethymnon had resulted in the deliverance of Freyberg's fleeing troops, as the German command had failed to realise that the main body of the Allied force was evacuating from the south in the fishing village at Sphakia. When the Allies had pulled back, Ringel had assumed they were retiring along the coast road towards Rethymnon, and although the bulk of the Luftwaffe had been withdrawn to prepare for the invasion of the Soviet Union, enough aerial reconnaissance remained for pilots to report there was no sign of the British to the east. In fact, significant forces were not sent south towards the port until 31 May.

In the meantime, scattered patrols of the 85th Gebirgs Regiment under Kampfgruppe Krakau, trying to follow the retreat south, had toiled through the mountains to outflank enemy positions guarding the Suda–Sphakia road, vital for the push eastwards and equally vital to the Allied withdrawal plan. On the night of 26–27 May the battle group occupied the heights above Stilos. As the Gebirgsjäger approached the town at about 06:30 the following morning, fire from a blocking position of artillery and tanks suddenly pinned it down. With a barrage of anti-tank weapons, artillery and mortar fire, the defence was breached. At 08:50 on 29 May, I Battalion of the 100th Gebirgsjäger Regiment (Kampfgruppe Utz) was sent southwards, and that afternoon II Battalion followed. The advance continued until 18:00, when a determined rearguard action was encountered just north of Kares. The attack was resumed in the morning and further progress was made to a point about two and a half miles from the coast. By the evening of 30 May the whole of Crete, except the Loutro–Sphakia area, was in German hands.

Above: Battalion command post in the mountains.

General Freyberg left the island that evening by flying boat. The Royal Navy evacuated almost 15,000 men to Egypt, with several ships damaged and sunk in the course of their operations. However, the Germans were unable to push down to the coast until 09:00 on 1 June, when the tenacious Allied rearguard forces finally surrendered. The war diary of the 5th Gebirgs Division recorded that the final resistance was overcome at 16:00 in the mountains north of Sphakia.

For Britain and its Allies, Crete was yet another stunning defeat. Hitler had secured his southern flank and gained a valuable staging ground for operations in the eastern Mediterranean. The British and Dominion casualties were more than 4,000 killed or wounded and 11,835 taken prisoner. Furthermore, the British naval presence in the theatre had been reduced to a skeleton by the loss of three cruisers and six destroyers sunk, and of one aircraft carrier, three battleships, six cruisers and nine destroyers damaged.

Yet it was in many ways a Pyrrhic victory for the Germans. Of the 22,000 men committed to the operation, approximately 6,000 were casualties. The 5th Gebirgs Division alone lost 20 officers and 305 other ranks killed in action. Of the 18 officers and 488 other ranks listed as missing, most were presumed drowned in the convoy attack. Nearly 271 of the 500 transport aircraft involved were lost, which was to have major ramifications in the forthcoming Russian campaign. Despite this enormous sacrifice, Hitler never pursued the opportunity to dominate the Eastern Mediterranean from Crete. Ringel offered a fitting epitaph: 'This sacrifice would have not been too great if the Crete campaign had meant a beginning, not an end.' In mid-July Student and Ringel flew to East Prussia to receive decorations for valour. Student was bluntly informed by the Führer that 'the days of the paratroop are over', and after Crete the German parachute arm was never used again in large-scale airborne operations.

Below: The Ju52 landings at Maleme were extremely dangerous – 80 of the aircraft were damaged as they landed as a result of heavy shelling.

LIECHTENSTEIN

With the formal cessation of hostilities on Crete, the 5th Gebirgs Division remained on the island as part of the occupying force. The role the division was scheduled to play in Operation 'Tyr', the planned invasion of the tiny mountain city-state of Liechtenstein, part of Hitler's plans for total European conquest, is not well known. (Contingency plans also existed for the takeover of Spain, Portugal, and Sweden.)

During the late 1930s Nazi agents provocateur failed in their attempts to subvert the plebiscite process in Liechtenstein and arouse calls for a union with Germany, as they had successfully done in Austria. As the tiny state posed no threat to the Nazi regime, it was left untouched.

Nonetheless, Hitler ordered plans be drawn up for the invasion of that country in May 1941. His astrologer had advised him that 'pebbles in the shoe can become boulders that roll and crush', and that Liechtenstein was key to that prophecy. Immediately, Hitler demanded a 'Liechtenstein Solution' from Field Marshal Keitel. Keitel acceded to the Führer's request, as usual, and delegated the planning to his chief of staff, General Jodl.

Above: Gebirgsjäger in summer uniform moving up a hillside on Crete.

Jodl felt insulted at having to plan an operation against a country as insignificant as Liechtenstein while being left out of most of the planning for 'Barbarossa'. He submitted Operation 'Tyr' calling for four divisions, justifying his numbers on the grounds the Swiss might renounce their neutrality and intervene on behalf of the mountain duchy. He requested the 1st and 4th Gebirgs Divisions from Army Group South, together with the 5th and 6th Gebirgs Divisions, which were both garrisoning Crete after the fierce campaigns there. The 188th Reserve Gebirgs Division, a training outfit based in northern Austria, would provide a garrison for the area.

Jodl submitted his plans, and Keitel delivered them to Hitler. The Führer swallowed whole Jodl's fantasies of Swiss intervention and approved the plan without modification. He ordered the divisions be brought up to crush Liechtenstein. As soon as they found out, Field Marshal Gerd von Rundstedt, commander of Army Group South, and General Ringel of the 5th Gebirgs Division who commanded the garrison in Crete, protested strongly about the commitment of their forces to such a pointless venture. Hitler would hear none of it and considered having them relieved of command. Only the vociferous objections of Halder and Field Marshals Leeb and Bock saved von Rundstedt from being dismissed. Ringel was currently riding on a crest of popularity after the Cretan campaign, and Hitler's staff recommended that he too be retained.

Nevertheless, the divisions prepared to move out to conquer Liechtenstein. The Cretan garrison was to be withdrawn first, as it would be the most difficult to extricate and other divisions would have to be sent in as replacements. Just before the transports loaded up the replacement units, an emergency cable arrived from Berlin: Operation 'Tyr' had been called off.

The reasons for its cancellation are still not entirely clear, but documents so far point to a change in the stars and a modification of the prophecy made by Hitler's astrologer. That the plan was suddenly abandoned is very clear. The 5th and 6th Gebirgs Divisions remained in Crete, and the 1st and 4th Gebirgs Divisions remained attached to Army Group South. Although Hitler expected to be able to execute Operation 'Tyr' in mid-1942, it was rapidly shelved. It was briefly dusted off in June 1943, in the overconfidence preceding the Kursk campaign, but in the wake of Germany's resounding defeat at Kursk it was consigned to the dustbin. Documents relating to this operation were only recently uncovered in a mass of German Army horsefeed requisitioning forms.

After moving to Germany between September and October, the 5th Gebirgs Division spent the winter of 1941–2 preparing for a move to the Eastern Front. On 16 October the *Armelband Kreta* or Crete cuff-title was instituted for those who had taken part in operations on Crete between 20 and 27 May 1941. Then, on 1 November, Aufklärungs Abteilung 95 and Panzerjäger Abteilung 95 were exchanged with the 3rd Gebirgs Division for Aufklärungs Abteilung 68 and Panzerjäger Abteilung 48, but these two battalions remained in Finland and were assigned as army troops on 5 January 1942.

EASTERN FRONT

The Battle of Leningrad
'When Operation "Barbarossa" is launched, the world will hold its breath!' said Adolf Hitler before German forces began their invasion of Russia on 22 June 1941. And so it did as he unleashed the mightiest army ever assembled on the ill-prepared Red forces. Initially the gains were stunning, but with the onset of the autumn rains, the assault faltered and halted along the whole 1,800 mile front, and his enemies breathed a collective sigh of relief.

Below: After the battle – a Gebirgsjäger relaxes with a trio of *Deutsches Rotes Kreuz* (DRK German Red Cross) nurses.

At the end of July, Hitler had given Leningrad (now St Petersburg) priority over Moscow as the most important objective of 'Barbarossa', and wanted to divert a panzer group from Army Group Centre to hasten the advance northward, but the OKW persuaded him to transfer only a corps. After considering the problem and arguing with his generals several weeks longer, Hitler announced his final decision on 21 August. He intended to give priority to the flanks, in the south taking the Crimea and the Donets Basin industrial region and cutting the Russians off from the Caucasus oil, and in the north taking Leningrad and joining forces with the Finns. Only after Leningrad had been secured and Army Group South was well on its way would the advance toward Moscow resume. In the meantime, Army Group Centre would divert strong forces to assist Army Group South to push southward into the Ukraine.

On the northern flank, fighting had been continuous through to 8 August when the Germans attacked Krasnogvardeisk. In the second half of August, the Finnish Army and Army Group North closed in rapidly on Leningrad. On 30 August Germans forces cut the rail-link to Moscow, isolating Leningrad off from the rest of Russia. On 31 August, the Finns reached their pre-1940 border on the Karelian Isthmus 30 miles north of Leningrad, and on the same day an Army Group North division arrived at the Neva River 10 miles southeast of the city. Four days later, the Finnish Army opened an offensive east of Lake Ladoga toward the Svir River, where it expected to make contact with German forces coming from the southwest.

On 8 September, Army Group North took Shlisselburg (or Schlüsselburg, in German) and with it the communication system, isolating Leningrad from the outside world. Already the only means of resupplying the city was by air drop or by crossing Lake Ladoga. By 9 September the Germans were within cannon range of the city, and when tanks broke through the last fortified line, which stood less than 10 miles from the outskirts, it appeared to all that Leningrad was doomed.

Below: Time out of combat wasn't all DRK nurses – here Gebirgsjäger are instructed on the intricacies of the Czech 7.92mm 26(t) light machine gun which was issued to some units instead of the MG34 or MG42.

Above: MG34 in the air defence role. (See pages 72–3.)

The city probably could have been taken in a few weeks despite exceptionally stiff Soviet resistance had it not been for several unusual circumstances. In the first place, Hitler decided that Leningrad was to be surrounded and not entered, and the army group therefore had to try to manoeuvre into the narrow isthmus to the east. Secondly, the Finnish commander in chief, Field Marshal (later Marshal of Finland) Baron Carl G. E. Mannerheim, refused to cross the border and close in from the north. Apparently he did not want to do what he conceived to be the Germans' work for them, and he also did not want to lend substance to the old Soviet argument that the Finnish border on the Karelian Isthmus was a threat to Leningrad. Finally, in the second week of September, Hitler removed Army Group North's armour. He left the army group one motorised corps, and demanded that it be withheld for a thrust toward the east to meet the Finns on the Svir when the time was ripe.

Hitler had decided on 6 September to concentrate German strength on Moscow after all. Army Group Centre was to be reinforced at the expense of its two neighbours, and Army Groups North and South were to complete their missions with the forces remaining to them. With the panzer units badly needed elsewhere, the OKW appealed to Hitler to institute a siege at Leningrad so that these units could be redeployed. On 29 September 1941, Hitler gave his approval to the plan. Furthermore, he ordered that the city be reduced so that the Germans would not have to feed its population. Thus began the epic siege of Leningrad, established on a line that began on the shore of the Gulf of Finland at Novoikerzon and curved eastward to Petergof and Uritsk, both within view of the city. Relentless shelling and air raids continued for the next 872 days, until Red Army troops finally drove away the German besiegers in mid-January 1944.

On 16 October 1942, Army Group North launched a limited attack across the Volkhov River toward Tikhvin and the Svir River, which the Finnish Army had reached at the end of September. After the first two or three days the autumn rains overtook the operation, and before the end of the first week the troops were leaving their tanks and trucks behind, bogged down on muddy roads. On 8 November German troops broke into Tikhvin, but there they stayed only until mid-December, when Russian units closing in on all sides forced them back to the Volkhov.

The Soviet winter offensive

During the summer and fall of 1941 the Soviet armies retreated because they had to and not (as was claimed as long as Stalin lived) because of a masterful strategic plan. The nation suffered staggering losses, including two-thirds of its pre-war coal-producing areas, three-quarters of its iron and manganese ore production, and 35 million people. Nevertheless, the sacrifices bought time, which the Soviet regime exploited with ruthless energy. Even while they were in full retreat, losing, destroying, or tearing down and shipping to the east entire industrial complexes, the Russians managed to recruit and equip fresh armies. As of 1 December, Soviet casualties probably totalled between 4 and 5 million men, but at the same time the Germans identified at or near the front 280 rifle and cavalry divisions and 44 tank or mechanised brigades.

The Soviet High Command did not share Hitler's doubts about the strategic importance of Moscow. In the summer and autumn it sacrificed entire armies and groups of armies in attempts to hold the western approaches to the capital. It would have sacrificed more in the battle for the city itself had not the earliest and coldest winter in half a century almost literally frozen the German armies in their tracks.

The long delays in August, September and October and the German loss of momentum on the northern and southern flanks in November had given the Russians time to assemble strong reserves around Moscow. Possibly, had the cold not set in, the German armies would have battled their way through that mass of men as they had

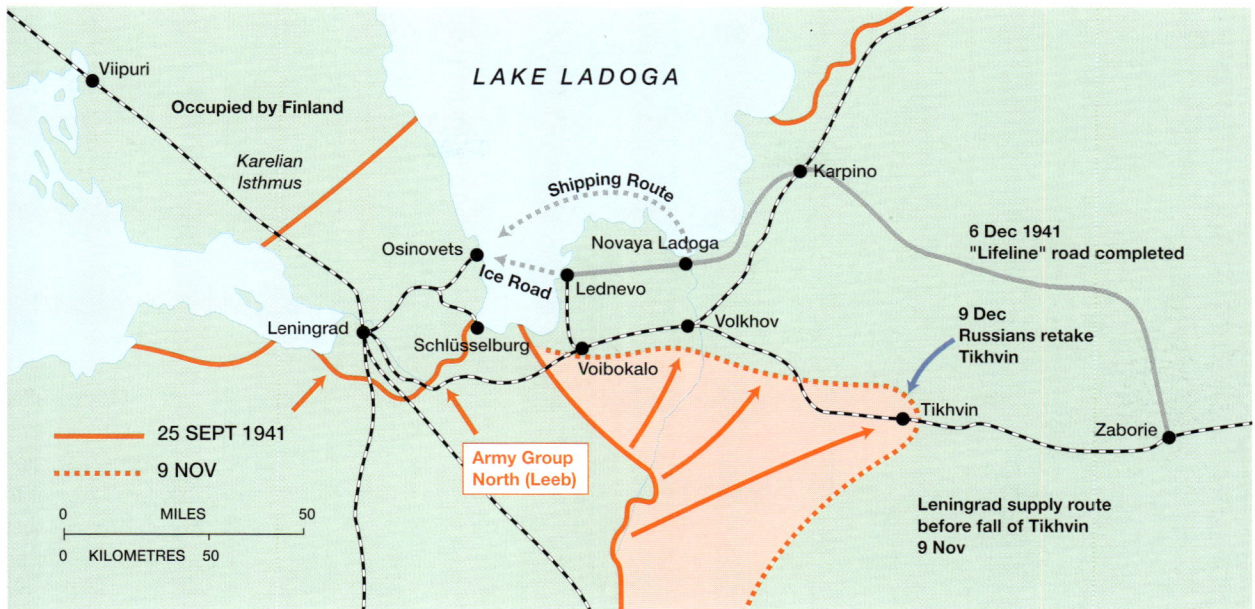

Above: The siege of Leningrad.

through others, but victory, as Bock predicted late in November, would have been achieved by the narrowest of margins. As it was, the German offensive ground to a halt on 5 December.

But as winter descended on the front the Soviets launched a mighty counteroffensive. The first stage, beginning on 6 December and lasting approximately a month, consisted of furious Russian attacks against Army Group Centre. These blows were to drive the Germans back from the gates of Moscow and, in so doing, destroy the advanced German panzer groups if possible. The attacks breached the thin German lines at several points and sent Hitler's armies reeling westward until a stand-fast order braked their retreat. By the end of December, the front had temporarily stabilised, with most German units on the central sector driven to a form of strongpoint defence.

Encouraged by the success of these first attacks, Stalin ordered an even greater counteroffensive effort on 5 January 1942. This second stage mounted major Soviet efforts against all three German army groups and aimed at nothing less than the total annihilation of the Wehrmacht's armies in Russia. Tearing open large gaps in the German front, Soviet armies advanced deep into the German rear and, in mid-January, created the most serious crisis yet. Grim reality finally succeeded where professional military advice had earlier failed, and Hitler at last authorised a large-scale withdrawal of the central German front on 15 January. Even with this concession, the German position in Russia remained in peril until Soviet attacks died out in late February.

The first stage of the Soviet winter counteroffensive drove the Germans back from Moscow but failed to destroy the advanced German panzer forces. The divisions of Army Group Centre adopted a strongpoint style of defence as they retreated.

When Hitler ordered the German armies to stand fast on 16 December, the opening Soviet drives had already spent much of their offensive energy and were unable to sustain their far-ranging attacks with supplies, replacements and fresh units.

During the latter part of December, both sides struggled to reinforce their battered forces. Hitler ordered the immediate dispatch of 13 fresh divisions to the Eastern Front from other parts of German-occupied Europe, including the 5th Gebirgs Division, although there was a considerable delay in the arrival of these reinforcements. In a curious parallel to Hitler's command actions, Soviet leader Joseph Stalin assumed

Above: Gebirgsjäger relax in their farmhouse billet; Russia 1942.

Right: This Gebirgsjäger Leutnant talking to the crew of a Panzer IV has a Bergführer (mountain leader) badge on his breast and a tank destruction badge on his right arm.

personal control over the strategic direction of Russian operations in late December. In Moscow, Stalin saw in the Red Army's surprising early success the makings of an even grander counteroffensive to crush the invaders and win the war at one stroke. Pushing Russian reinforcements forward as fast as they could be assembled, Stalin sketched out his new vision for this second stage of the Soviet counteroffensive. The Leningrad, Volkhov and Northwestern Fronts would smash in the front of Army Group North and lift the siege of Leningrad. The Kalinin, Western and Bryansk Fronts would annihilate Army Group Centre by a colossal double envelopment. In the south, the Soviet Southwestern and Southern Fronts would crush Army Group South, while the Caucasus Front undertook amphibious landings to regain the Crimea.

This Red Army avalanche fell on the Germans during the first two weeks of January, thus beginning the second stage of the winter campaign. The objectives were far too ambitious and greatly exceeded what could be done with Red Army resources. The attacking Soviet armies managed to penetrate the German strongpoint belt in several areas, but once into the German rear, they had not sufficient strength or impetus to achieve a decisive victory.

As part of this ambitious offensive, during the winter Marshal Meretskov's Volkhov Front repeatedly tried to break through the blockade of Leningrad. His orders of 17 December 1941 were to smash German armies on the west bank of the Volkhov River and gave the 2nd Soviet Shock Army, commanded by General A. A. Vlasov, the main task of breaching through defence line on the west bank.

Vlasov made the area south of Kirishi on the River Volkhov the focus of his attack. Here, the terrain was predominantly swamp and primeval forest, making military operations difficult in winter (and well nigh impossible in the summer months). On 13 January, while there was still frozen ground enough to manoeuvre, the Second Shock Army ripped through the German lines to the south of the 254th Infantry

Above: Refreshment break – note the ankle boots and canvas gaiters rather than the usual German Army jackboots.

Division. By 20 January the breach had been expanded to a width of nearly 20 miles. Vlasov's forces advanced through the breach and began to move in a northeasterly direction. By mid-February, after advancing over 60 miles, they had reached the Lyuban area and had thus covered half the distance to Leningrad. However, the advance was hampered by the lack of reserves and materiel resources (tanks, ammunition, self-propelled artillery and the rest), and a general lack of coordination between the Leningrad and Volkhov Fronts. By the end of February, Stalin's great offensive had run its course.

The German forces too were restricted by the terrain, a lack of reserves and Soviet attacks on other parts of the front, forcing them to take individual battalions from their parent divisions and commit them in ad-hoc battle groups in an attempt to build up a defensive front. But having vehicles and a good network of roads, they could manoeuvre these groups and concentrate them on the spearheads of the Soviet drive. By early March, a stable defensive line had been formed. For the next three months fierce combat ensued all around the salient, with the Soviets striving to expand their gains and the Germans attempting to halt them, and also to cut Second Shock Army off from its supply.

In early March, the 5th Gebirgs Division was transferred to I Corps in the Eighteenth Army of Army Group North and moved into positions southwest of Leningrad, in the area east of Lyuban, where it would stay to fight a series of defensive battles until November of the following year. The flat, swampy terrain was wholly different from anything that it had trained or fought in up to this time.

Destruction of the Volkhov 'Kessel'

The arrival of the spring thaw turned the area into a vast, mosquito-infested swamp, to the total misery of both German and Soviet troops. The front line stood as stark evidence of the confused winter fighting: instead of spanning the front in a smooth arc marred by a few minor indentations, it snaked tortuously back and forth, its great swoops and bends marking the limits of Russian offensive and German defensive endurance.

The most conspicuous point was the narrow but long salient that had been created by the advance of General Vlasov's Second Shock Army: the Volkhov Front. As a result of German counterattacks, by 26 March Vlasov's forces – which included the 372nd Rifle Division, 24th and 58th Rifle Brigades, 4th and 24th Guards Rifle Divisions and 7th Tank Brigade – were in danger of encirclement. Another advance on 9 April by the SS Polizei Division to the southwest of Spasskaya Polist finally cut off the Soviet salient. In the 'Kessel' (cauldron or encircled area) were troops of seven rifle divisions, each of them numbering between 18,000 and 20,000 troops.

Then, on 22 May the Germans launched a final operation designed to eliminate the Second Shock Army, and by the morning of 6 June had driven between 59th and 52nd Soviet armies attempting to relieve the pocket. The 5th Gebirgs Division, to the northeast of the trapped forces, countered efforts by the 54th Army to drive southwest into the pocket via Lyuban. Fierce fighting in the primeval swamps and forests continued for the next month, but on 24 June communication with the staff of Second Shock Army was interrupted. Finally, on 12 July, General Vlasov surrendered 30,000 of his men into captivity.

Above: The ski stretcher for casualty recovery was standard mountain troops' equipment and was handled by a four-man team as seen here. (See also page 75.)

Lake Ladoga

On 7 April, Red Army troops managed to force a very narrow corridor to Leningrad, opening a tenuous rail link to the city. Trains ran into the city with desperately needed supplies and came out with civilians and the wounded, all under heavy artillery fire from the Germans. Soon, however, this link was cut and Leningrad was once again isolated.

In the late spring and early summer of 1942, the 5th Gebirgs Division was tasked with clearing out the various pockets of resistance that remained at large after the crushing defeat of the Second Shock Army. The terrain, covered with mile after mile of heavy, dank, pine forests, provided ample places to hide and favoured the prey. Hitler's Directive No 44 (Operations in Northern Finland) of 21 July 1942 makes it clear that the division was intended for the 20th Mountain Army in Finland 'by the end of September', but this was based on the assumption that 'Leningrad will be captured in September at the latest'. But the Soviet forces showed no signs of relinquishing the city. On 24 August they launched another major offensive to relieve it. On 27 August the offensive expanded to an attack by the Leningrad Front in the city and the Volkhov Front outside the siege lines. Both fronts were aimed against the German positions at Schlüsselburg on Lake Ladoga. The 5th Gebirgs Division was rushed into positions to counter the mighty blows, and successfully withstood a series of human wave assaults. On 10 September, after taking heavy losses in attack, the Red Army forces halted their operations for the winter as rains once again made movement nearly impossible.

1943

Beginning on 1 January 1943, there were renewed attacks on the German positions in the Pogoste Kessel and south of Kolpino, as a result of which the 5th Gebirgs Division moved to shore up the defences on the Neva at Kolpino. Then, on the 12th, Operation 'Iskra' (Spark) hit the narrow sector of the southern coast of Ladoga Lake. Strengthened by reserves, the armies of the Volkhov and Leningrad Fronts, supported by the 13th and 14th Air Armies and artillery of the Baltic fleet and Ladozhskaya flotilla, struck from two directions at the German defences. Although the German troops offered strong resistance, the defence was pierced at the Mga–Sinyavsk projection, and after seven days of bitter fighting the Germans were driven back some six miles from the southern coast of Lake Ladoga. The blockade of Leningrad was finally broken by Soviet troops on 18 January 1943, when Schlüsselburg was liberated. By the end of the month a railway was built on the corridor that now connected Leningrad with the mainland. Supplies were rushed into the city while wounded and non-combatants were shipped out. All of this was done under constant artillery fire against the cordon. A week later the Soviet leadership announced that the siege of Leningrad was raised. For the first time in many days, the populace could walk openly in the streets without fear of air attack.

Despite this, rations in the city were still very limited, and German artillery was still in range of any part of the city. Because of the shortages in food and supplies, an offensive to break the blockade was impossible. Attempts to widen the corridor (only six miles wide) failed at a heavy cost in men and matériel.

Between November 1941 and October 1942 alone, 641,803 people died of starvation in Leningrad.

Operation 'Polar Star'

Between 15 and 28 February the Soviets tried to consolidate their newly won positions by a series of limited thrusts. The main attack was on the Demyansk salient (Operation 'Polar Star'), where six German divisions of II and X Army Corps were entrenched. By 23 February the Soviet formations had penetrated only 6–10 miles, by which time the bulk of the German forces had been withdrawn through the tightening noose.

In the second half of March, further attempts were made to continue the offensive in the direction of Sinyavsk–Mga. As part of LIV Corps in the Eighteenth Army, the 5th Gebirgs Division was committed to a series of defensive actions near Novgorod, during which time a light reconnaissance detachment (95th Schnelle Abteilung) was attached to the division. In the middle of April the German forces southeast of Leningrad launched a series of counterattacks, but these were swiftly put down by the Soviet Fourteenth Army. Then, on 14 May, a fresh attempt was made to cut the land bridge to Leningrad, but this operation too quickly fell apart.

Throughout the summer German operations around Leningrad continued to vacillate between defence and attack. In late July another Soviet attack fell on the German positions on the Mga, the purpose of which was to disrupt German plans to organise a new offensive on Leningrad and tie down their forces in the area. In the face of this new onslaught all reserves of Lindemann's Eighteenth Army and significant forces from other front areas were committed, including the 5th Gebirgs Division Although their defences held fast, after a month of fighting the Germans had incurred heavy losses, most of them from artillery fire and aircraft attacks. Some of the most serious losses were incurred by the fire-brigade units such as the 5th Gebirgs, which was all but destroyed in these battles.

Mga offensive

When in September the Soviet armies took possession of the powerful defences near Sinyavsk, the staff of Army Group North recognised that their positions on the Volkhov had become precarious. In October German troops were removed from their positions on the river through the Kirishi bridgehead and rearranged in newly constructed defences.

On 7 October another setback occurred when the Red Army launched a fresh offensive at Nevel. By the end of December the army group comprised only 40 incomplete divisions, defending a front extending 500 miles. Permission was urgently sought to withdraw from Leningrad and move west to the 'Panther Line'. Although such movement offered the chance to shorten the defence line by 120 miles, Hitler rejected the request.

Already, the 5th Gebirgs Division had received the welcome news that it was to leave the Eastern Front for Italy, where the Allied campaign was slowly gathering momentum, First however, it was transferred to the reserve of Generaloberst von Vietinghoff's Tenth Army of Army Group C (Kesselring) in northern Italy to rest and refit.

It was a much-needed furlough for the Gebirgsjäger, as the battles in which they had fought in the past months were some of the bloodiest and most wasteful of the war, with neither side able to make appreciable gain despite monumental sacrifice. Indeed, the Leningrad

Below: Winter transport for a 10.5cm leichte Feldhaubitze 16 being horse-drawn in the snow on a wood skid in northern Russia. The men are wearing the two-piece winter suit and the horses have white camouflage sheeting.

Front has since come to symbolise the horrors of the Eastern Front. During the siege, starvation claimed hundreds of thousands of lives but, incredibly, war production continued in Leningrad's bombed-out factories, even through the frozen winter. In many ways the failure of the German offensive can be attributed to actions elsewhere, particularly at Stalingrad, which consumed resources needed to carry the offensive.

Though the Germans would never take Leningrad the defence of the city would be one of the costliest for Russia in the war.

MONTE CASSINO AND THE GUSTAV LINE

After the Axis retreat and Allied victory on the island of Sicily, in the autumn of 1943 the Allies had landed uncontested on the mainland of Italy, the so-called 'soft underbelly of Europe', at Reggio and Taranto. After further landings at Salerno timed to coincide with the Italian armistice, Kesselring sent the 16th Panzer Division to the Salerno area to meet the invasion, and mobilised the Tenth Army behind it to help drive the Allied force back into the sea. By 16 September, Vietinghoff was forced to concede that the Allies were not to be dislodged from the Salerno beachhead. He began a phased withdrawal, satisfied in the knowledge that he had disrupted the timetable for the capture of Naples. As they withdrew the Germans demolished everything that could not be shipped north, while engineers began to construct a series of defensive lines across the Italian peninsula. The first of these, Viktor, began 18 miles north of Naples, next came the Barbara and Bernhardt Lines and finally the Gustav. Kesselring believed that this could be made almost impregnable and prevent the Allies from reaching Rome for many months.

Above: Mountain troops' observation post, with winter camouflaged binocular sight.

The terrain certainly favoured the defenders, as running down the spine of Italy is the long Apennine range, at its highest point rising to 6,000 ft. From it a series of ridges and valleys radiate out onto narrow coastal strips – only 25 miles wide on the west side and 10 miles on the east. Even in good weather the roads were barely adequate for motorised columns and supply convoys. In winter they would become quagmires, dictating that the war would have to be waged by foot soldiers, fighting mile by mile.

Through the late autumn and into the winter months Vietinghoff slowly withdrew through the prepared positions. On 15 November the worsening weather forced General Alexander, commander of the Allied Fifth Army Group, to call a halt to the advance. By the time he was ready to resume the advance, the Germans were firmly entrenched on the Gustav defensive line in expectation of the allied offensive.

The Gustav Line

The Gustav Line ran across the width of central Italy, from the mouth of the Sangro River in the east, through the Abruzzi mountain region to the mouths of the Rapido/Garigliano Rivers on the west coast. The dominating feature on the defensive line was a defile on which stood the town of Cassino. Less than a thousand yards west of Cassino town is Monte Cassino, towering 1,700 ft above the town. On top of Monte Cassino stood the centuries-old Benedictine monastery, the scene of many battles over the years. It dominated the surrounding countryside, including the Liri valley that ran through the mountains to the north and Route 6, the main highway linking the south to Rome, which snaked around Monastery Hill.

To defend Cassino and the Gustav Line Vietinghoff, newly promoted to Generaloberst, had 15 divisions including the 44th Infantry Division (Generalleutnant Ortner) and the 5th Gebirgs Division (Generalleutnant Schrank), which in January was attached to XIV Corps and moved into positions on the Gustav Line south of Rome. Added to this was the 1st Fallschirmjäger Division (Generalleutnant Heidrich) of LI Mountain Corps

Above: Wearing 1939-pattern anoraks in both camouflage and plain pattern, this infantry ski company moves up to positions in the Gothic Line.

(General der Gebirgstruppen Feuerstein); this brought together the paratroops and the Gebirgsjäger who had fought together in Crete two years previously. Under XIV Panzer Corps (Generalleutnant von Senger und Etterlin) were the 71st Infantry Division (Generalmajor Raapke), 94th Infantry Division (Generalmajor Steinmetz) and the 15th Panzergrenadier Division (Generalmajor Rodt).

Facing the Cassino front the allies now had seven Commonwealth divisions, containing men from India, New Zealand, South Africa (who had an armoured division in reserve) and Brazil, as well as five American, five British, four French and three Polish divisions. On the eastern flank, LI Mountain Corps faced forces of the British Eighth Army. In the west, XIV Panzer Corps, by this point desperately short of tanks and heavily reliant its infantry units, faced the US Fifth Army.

The Allies faced an ominous task, as along the whole front German engineers had made very skilful use of terrain to fortify their positions. Mines were planted on the roads and trails, at the heads of gullies and in the natural cross-country approaches. All bridges and culverts were destroyed, and sites for bypasses were mined. Machine-gun and mortar emplacements, many of them dug four or five feet into solid rock, covered nearly every path. Not even intense artillery concentrations could smash these positions. On the slopes of mountains, behind stream beds, and across narrow valleys, dozens of mutually supporting machine guns were sited to weave a deadly pattern of cross fire. As a result of these defences, small forces of the enemy could hold the gullies, draws and difficult trails that led into the mountains, even in the face of strong attacks. To further impede the Allied advance, the countryside in front of the Rapido east of Cassino town had been flooded.

Allied attacks on the Gustav Line commenced on 15 December, with coordinated attacks by II Corps in the San Pietro area and by VI Corps in the mountains to the north.

The main objectives were the heights north of Cassino at the head of the Rapido River Valley, but between lay 10 miles of rugged mountain country.

VI Corps' offensive opened with an attack toward the village of Lagone, which fell on 16 December. Just to the north of Lagone, fighting on 15 and 16 December brought the first contact with the 5th Gebirgs Division. Before daybreak on the 15th, the 1st Platoon of the 45th Reconnaissance Troop ventured out on a volunteer mission to capture Hill 895, held by elements of the 100th Gebirgs Regiment. Although the Gebirgsjäger broke up the platoon's assault, their hold along this sector was weakened. After dark a platoon of Company C, 179th Infantry, was able to take La Bandita without opposition, and the next day the 100th Gebirgs Regiment was forced to yielded Hill 895 to French troops of the 5th Rifle Regiment.

On 17 December all the German front-line units on VI Corps' front began a general withdrawal. Though the penetrations were nowhere deep enough to cause great alarm, the positions had become increasingly difficult to hold. It was therefore decided to make a limited withdrawal, regroup on a new line, and thus gain a breathing spell. A withdrawal would also lengthen the enemy supply lines through the mountains and bring him into new and unfamiliar terrain.

The first battle

The next concerted assault on the Gustav Line was launched on 17 January 1944, in coordination with the landings at Anzio planned for the 22nd. The British X Corps was to cross the Garigliano River west of Cassino and try to outflank German positions around the Liri Valley. The French Expeditionary Force was to move through the mountains in the east and complete a flanking manoeuvre. In the centre, the US II Corps would cross the Rapido River a few miles south of Cassino and enter the Liri Valley.

In support of the Allied assault, troops from the French 3rd Algerian Division struck the 5th Gebirgs Division and 8th Panzergrenadier Regiment positions on Mt Belvedere, flanking Cassino. Meeting heavy resistance, they were quickly checked, while to the west the British were halted and failed to execute the western flanking manoeuvre. With neither objective met, the Allied troops dug in around the hills and mountains around Monte Cassino.

Two days into the operation, the US 36th Division assaulted across the Rapido. The going was unexpectedly tough in the fast-flowing, steep-sided river, and many boats and their occupants were lost in the crossing. Those men who reached the other side of the river established a small bridgehead, but as the sun rose artillery fire was brought down on them from positions on Monte Cassino. Through the next night, more bridges were built across the Rapido to reinforce the bridgehead, but still they were held at bay. On 22 January, as the division's casualties escalated, the order was given to pull back. Two days later, the US 34th Division crossed the Rapido east of Cassino to try and outflank German positions. Over the next few days they advanced to within a few hundred yards of Monastery Hill, but again at a heavy cost, and were unable to approach any closer to Monte Cassino.

With this first assault on the Cassino front of the Gustav Line repulsed, it seemed that Kesselring's maxim, that the British and Americans would 'break their teeth' on the Gustav Line would ring true. But already the Axis commander faced another problem, for on 22 January, British and Americans under command of the US VI Corps had carried out an almost unopposed landing on beaches at Anzio, 60 miles to the north. This landing behind the German lines was designed to draw German forces away from the Cassino front, and thus weaken the Gustav Line defences. The Allied forces on the Cassino front could then head north and link up with the US VI Corps before advancing on their goal, Rome. However, contrary to expectations, parts of the newly reconstituted German

Below: The 8cm Granatwerfer 34 was the standard mortar for mountain troops, as with other German fighting units.

Above: Gebirgsjäger regimental HQ with commander and senior staff housed in a *mittlerer Kraftomnibus* command vehicle built by Magirus.

Fourteenth Army, which had been taking part in the occupation of northern Italy, were rushed to Anzio. Although only two German battalions stood between Anzio and Rome, VI Corps chose to consolidate their beachhead before attempting a breakout. This was quickly contained, and stalemate set in. There would be no easy road to Rome.

During this lull, command of the 5th Gebirgs Division passed on 10 February to Generalleutnant Max Schrank, who was to hold the position until January 1945. The highly popular and respected Generalleutnant Ringel, who had led the division through Greece, Crete and Russia, was promoted to the command of LXIX Mountain Corps.

The second and third battles

Focus returned to the Cassino Front where, on 14 February, leaflets were dropped onto the monastery informing the occupants and refugees that the allies had decided to bomb it and the surrounding German positions from the air. Up to this point both sides had tacitly agreed to avoid the destruction of Italy's historical assets unless it was a military necessity. However, many Allied troops, chief among them the commander of the New Zealand II Corps, General Freyberg, insisted that the destruction of the monastery was indeed necessary, and Alexander felt forced to assent. On the next day wave after wave of heavy bombers, acting in a tactical role, pulverised the monastery with heavy bombs. This highly controversial attack drew condemnation from all sides, and succeeded only in turning the monastery into a fortress; the ruined walls, which had been up to 15 ft thick, made excellent defensive positions which the Germans quickly occupied.

Following the aerial barrage, the second battle of Cassino began in earnest as US and Commonwealth troops attacked key points on the approaches to the battered monastery. After four days of fierce fighting the assault was called off. The survivors dug in, some of them only yards from the enemy dugouts and as heavy snow and freezing rain forced another break in the fighting, they watched nervously for the next attack.

On the morning of 15 March, as spring weather broke out over the bloodied slopes, another Allied bombardment fell on the German positions. When this ceased, the Fallschirmjäger holding the hill beat off an attack by 2nd New Zealand Division. Although tanks were sent in, they got bogged down in shell craters and mud and could only be used as static artillery.

The next morning, the monastery was again bombed, but the defenders remained largely untouched in their underground bunkers. Now being supplied solely by air drops, they continued to put up a determined resistance. On 19 March the Allied high command ordered yet another push to take German strong points in the town, and a frontal assault on Monte Cassino from Hangmans Hill by Gurkhas. It was hoped that tanks, which were being brought in on a newly carved track north of Cassino, would back up this assault. However, the advance on the town was kept at bay by tenacious German defenders, using tanks which had been half buried in the house ruins. By the afternoon the frontal assault was called off, and the Allied troops once again prepared to dig in around Monte Cassino. Only a week after the operation had started, the Allies had already lost 3,000 men.

Cassino was by now a pressing issue, for it had already been decided that the Gustav Line had to be broken before the Normandy invasion, planned for June, could take place. The Allies had to try and smash as many German divisions as they could, and rob Hitler of men that could be used in France.

And so another assault was planned for May. Parts of the British Eighth Army on the Adriatic front of the Gustav Line were secretly moved westward to the Cassino front. Fortunately for the Allies, the code-breakers at Bletchley Park were intercepting coded messages, which they read with the Enigma machine, and which contained details of the under-strength German formations facing them.

A four-pronged attack was planned, with the US II Corps attempting a breakthrough along the west coast following Route 7 and heading north in an attempt to link up with the US V Corps, who were attempting to break out of the Anzio beachhead.

The French Expeditionary Force of four divisions was to advance north through the Liri Valley, attacking German positions in the areas behind Monte Cassino. The British VIII Corps was to cross the Rapido River, clear the town and advance across the Gustav Line, cutting off the road west of Cassino. The Polish II Corps, comprising two infantry divisions and one armoured, had Monte Cassino as its objective. It was to encircle the mountain and attack from the north, first taking the German positions on Calvary Hill behind it.

At Cassino, the 1st Fallschirmjäger Division regrouped in preparation for the assault. The 5th Gebirgs Division was positioned some 10 miles north of Cassino and tasked with holding the line against the opposing Italian Motor Group (X Corps, Eighth Army). On Schrank's left flank, the 114th Jäger Division faced the 24th Guards Brigade and 4th Indian Division.

The final battle

Late in the evening of 11 May, 2,000 artillery pieces began to bombard the German positions on Cassino. Within an hour Polish forces were on Calvary Hill, just over 1,000 yards northwest of Cassino. The next day, pontoon bridges were constructed across the Rapido. The British VIII Corps crossed and advanced four miles, while the French Expeditionary Force moved up the Liri Valley. As the US II Corps thrust northwards up the coast towards Anzio, the German position began to deteriorate rapidly.

Another armoured assault on 16 May by Polish forces secured Calvary

Below: Gebirgsjäger moving into positions near Monte Cassino.

Above: The fourth and final battle for Monte Cassino – the Italian Front as at 11 May 1944.

Hill behind Monte Cassino, threatening the German line of retreat. With Allied forces now pouring through gaps in the line and bypassing German positions, Kesselring decided he could delay no longer and ordered the withdrawal from positions in the town, monastery, and surrounding hills and mountains. Thousands of German troops began an orderly retreat northwards on Route 6, the main highway linking the south to Rome. In failing to cut the highway, the Allies missed a sterling opportunity to score a major victory.

The town of Cassino finally fell on 17 May to Polish troops. The next day the Polish flag flew over the ruins where so many men had sacrificed their lives. Altogether the Germans had suffered 20,000 casualties in the defence of the Gustav Line, but their sacrifice had seriously delayed the Allied advance in Italy.

ROME

Between Rome and the Gustav Line, the Germans had constructed two delaying positions. The first, the Hitler/Dora Line, was sited six miles behind the Gustav Line and had been built to contain any forces that managed to break through the main position. It was half a mile deep, and laid with minefields, anti-tank traps, barbed wire and pillboxes. Behind this line a third defensive position, situated in the Alban Hills 20 miles south of Rome and named the Caesar Line, was under construction, but this was never finished.

Neither position could stem the Allied advance and both were quickly breached, forcing the German Tenth Army to make further withdrawals north and the Fourteenth

Army to retreat eastwards to avoid the Allied forces advancing from Anzio. During the retreat they destroyed bridges, laid mines on roads and prepared ambushes, all designed to delay the advancing Allied forces.

On 23 May, the US VI Corps finally broke out of the beachhead at Anzio, and two days later linked up with the US II Corps, advancing up the Liri Valley. The German Fourteenth Army at Anzio and the Tenth Army, withdrawing from their defensive positions, were partially encircled by this joint US force as they moved north, but avoided encirclement when it was decided that the Americans would head for Rome, which they then entered in triumph on 4 June 1944. Even as they paraded victoriously through the streets, German forces were slipping past the outskirts of Rome, heading north.

By the end of the first week of August 1944, members of the British Eighth Army stood on the Ponte Vecchio, bridging the Arno River in recently liberated Florence. The Eighth Army had just completed a campaign, in conjunction with the US Fifth Army, that had kept Axis forces in Italy in full retreat. For the first time since the Italian campaign had begun, Allied leaders were optimistic that they were on the verge of pushing the Germans out of the northern Apennines and sweeping through the Po Valley beyond. After that, many hoped for a rapid advance into the Alps, the Balkans, and perhaps into Austria, before winter and the enemy could stem their advance.

THE GOTHIC LINE

Axis forces, however, were preparing to frustrate any continuation of the Allied drive by building another belt of fortifications, the Gothic Line.

The new line generally consisted of a series of fortified passes and mountaintops, some 15 to 30 miles in depth north of the Arno River. It stretched for 200 miles from La Spezia on the Ligurian Sea through the Apennines, Pisa and Florence, to Pesaro on the east coast.

Along the Adriatic coast where the northern Apennines sloped down onto a broad coastal plain, the Gothic Line defences were generally anchored on the numerous rivers, streams and other waterways that flow from the mountains to the sea. One key to the line appeared to be the central Italian city of Bologna, a major rail and road communications hub located only a few miles north of the defensive belt.

The intense combat operations of the summer were not destined to continue into the fall. With the liberation of Rome on 4 June, and the invasion of Normandy two days later (Operation 'Overlord'), Allied resources earmarked for Italian operations, already considered of secondary importance, steadily diminished. The Allied invasion of southern France (Operation 'Anvil-Dragoon') on 15 August further reduced the limited resources available for the Italian theatre. More important, 'Anvil-Dragoon' stripped the Allied armies in Italy of seven first-class divisions, three American and four French.

Despite this scaling down the Allies planned to continue offensive operations in the northern Apennines in the hope of breaking through the Gothic Line and advancing into northern Italy. A continuation of the offensive, they hoped, would at least prevent the Germans from transferring their forces in Italy elsewhere.

Operations

In August 1944, Kesselring's Army Group C faced a still formidable Allied force. Field Marshal Alexander's command included troops from 16 Allied nations; Lieutenant General Mark W. Clark's Fifth Army (IV Corps and II Corps) held the western portion of the Allied line, from the Ligurian Sea at the mouth of the Arno River to a point just west of Florence. To the east Lieutenant General Sir Oliver Leese's larger Eighth Army, consisting of the Polish II Corps (two divisions), the Canadian I Corps (two divisions), the

British V Corps (six divisions), the British X Corps (two divisions), and the British XIII Corps (three divisions), held the line from the Florence area to just south of Fano on the Adriatic coast.

Opposing Clark's Fifth Army was Generalleutnant Joachim Lemelsen's Fourteenth Army, which contained 10 divisions belonging to I Parachute and XIV Panzer Corps. To the east, opposing the British Eighth Army, was the Tenth Army commanded by General Heinrich von Vietinghoff. This army consisted of 12 divisions belonging to LXXVI Panzer and LI Mountain Corps, which included the 5th Gebirgs Division. The two other Axis forces in northern Italy, the Ligurian Army and the Adriatic Command, controlled four more divisions and generally performed anti-partisan and reserve missions.

Operation 'Olive'

Soon after British forces reached the Arno River on 4 August 1944, planning for the next phase of the Allied attack had begun. Under this operation, code-named Olive, General Leese's army was to attack up the Adriatic coast to Rimini. Once this attack had drawn Axis units away from the Fifth Army's front, General Clark could hit the Gothic Line in a secondary assault from Florence directly north toward Bologna with his more limited force. The Fifth and Eighth Armies could then converge on and capture Bologna and move to encircle and destroy Axis forces in the Po Valley, putting Eighth Army forces in a favourable position to move into the Balkans and the Danube Valley.

Below: When radio silence demanded — or when atmospheric necessities dictated — mountain troops used signal flags.

The shift of British forces over battle-damaged and circuitous mountain routes to their start positions began on 15 August, while Fifth Army units maintained pressure on their front to convince the German commanders that the main thrust was coming in the Florence area. The movement, made easier by the almost total lack of German air reconnaissance, took all the following week; by 22 August, however, 11 divisions and nine separate brigades faced the German forces that were holding a 25-mile-wide stretch of the Gothic Line anchored on the Adriatic.

German radio communications and order-of-battle reports, intercepted and decrypted by ULTRA code-breakers in July and August, revealed to Alexander, Clark and Leese that neither Kesselring nor any of his subordinates had detected the eastward shift of Fifth Army and Eighth Army units. Similarly, the Axis command did not realise that a change in Allied operational strategy had occurred or that an attack along the coast was imminent.

Operation 'Olive' commenced on 25 August 1944, as the British V Corps and Canadian I Corps attacked through two Polish divisions on a 17-mile front along the Adriatic. The 5th Gebirgs Division was holding positions on the right against the 9th British Armoured Brigade, with 71st Infantry Division to their left and 278th Infantry Division holding the coast. The offensive, supported by the British Desert Air Force, rapidly gained ground, with the Canadian 5th Armoured Division in the centre moving far forward against light resistance. Polish and Canadian troops penetrated the Gothic Line near the coastal town of Pesaro on 30 August, threatening to turn the entire Axis front.

Originally believing that the Eighth Army assault was a diversion to draw troops from central Italy, Kesselring delayed steps to reinforce units on the coast for four days. However, the heroic resistance displayed by units such the 100th Gebirgsjäger Regiment (see below), maximising the defensive advantages provided by inclement weather and numerous rivers and ridges, inflicted a total of 8,000 casualties on the attackers and stalled Eighth Army forces short of their Rimini and Romagna Plain objectives by 3 September. The same cautiousness that had characterised previous Eighth Army engagements began to play to Kesselring's advantage, and he managed to plug the breach with rapidly mobilised reinforcements.

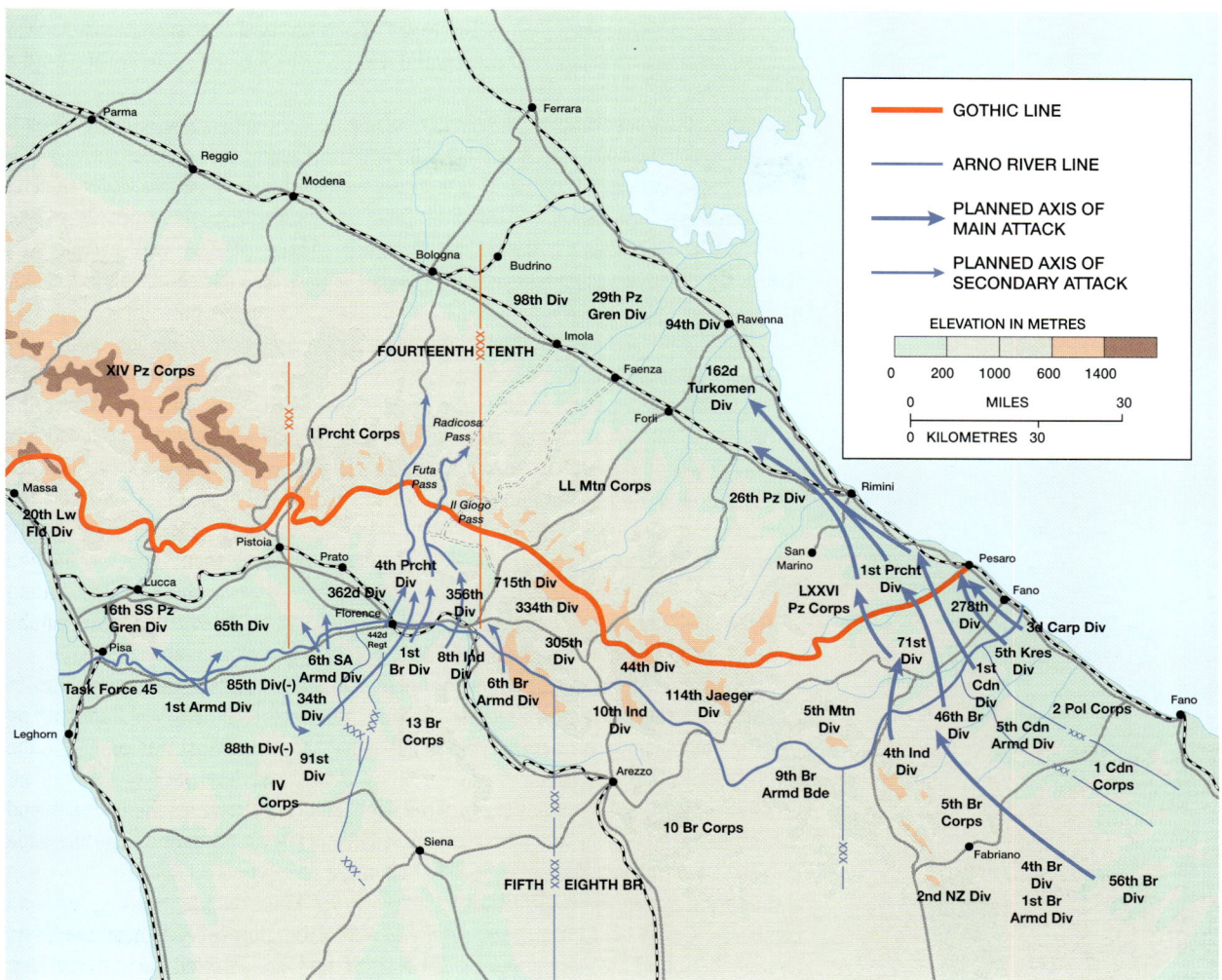

Above: The Allies attack the Gothic Line – Operation 'Olive', 25 August 1944.

Gemmano

When news of the breakthrough at Pesaro came through, 100th Regiment was deployed in Emilia-Romagna, holding a sector of the Galla Placidia anti-landing line between Rimini and Cesena. At that time the regiment, under the command of Oberstleutnant Richard Ernst, consisted of three Gebirgsjäger Battalions under Hauptmanns Hermann and Bachmaier and Major Zwickenpflug, and four fighting companies (reconnaissance, artillery, engineers and anti-tank), with a total of about 4,500 men.

On 1 September the regiment received orders to move to the River Conca valley and was put under the orders of the 71st Infantry Division, whose commander, General Raapke, ordered it to garrison a salient in the line at Gemmano. From 4 to 14 September, 100th Regiment fought tooth and nail against British Empire forces for the key points of the battlefront: Gemmano, Borgo, San Francesco height, Monte Gardo (Point 449), and Zollara were taken, lost and retaken at least 10 times by the combatants. The Gebirgsjägers' stubborn defence in the face of almost continuous attacks, often in close combat, became an epic in the German military history. A week into the battle German news radio broadcast the following dramatic announcement:

In the hard defensive fighting on the Adriatic, in the sector of Gemmano, the 100th Mountain Regiment, under the orders of Oberstleutnant Ernst, together with an artillery group under his orders, with its indestructible firmness and gallant counterattacks has behaved particularly well.

Three days later, following an order to withdraw to Montescudo, the last two German soldiers (one of whom was Ernst himself) left the Gemmano battlefront. The valour demonstrated during the battle of Gemmano earned the regiment no fewer than six *Ritterkreuz des Eisernes Kreuz* (Knight's Cross of the Iron Cross) awards as well as hundreds of Iron Crosses. The action for which August Rappel was awarded the Ritterkreuz, highly unusual for a common soldier, is described here by Ernst:

Rappel defended his blockhouse, then ejected the British from another blockhouse, then recaptured his own blockhouse, which had fallen to the enemy. Later he gave to his own artillery the order to fire against the positions, his own and those of the enemies, who were obliged to retire. And when a shell set fire to his blockhouse he saved his comrades from the flaming house. At last, when the flames were burnt out, he returned to the blockhouse.

When the battle was over, Ernst penned this epitaph for Gemmano:

How much blood this unhappy heap of ruins has drunk! Even if this waste of men had not the proportions of Cassino, the fighting here had the same obstinacy; with the same rage we fought for every house, for every ruin. And as Cassino was the tomb of the 1st Fallschirmjäger Division, so Gemmano was the tomb of my Regiment.

Exhausted by the tough battles on the Arno River and Gothic Line, at the end of August the 5th Gebirgs Division was placed on the reserve of the Ligurian Army and moved to the Western Alps (Alps Maritime). In September, the division was transferred to General der Gebirgstruppen Hans Schlemmer's LXXV Army Corps which, together with the Lombardy Corps of General der Artillerie Kurt Jahn, formed the Ligurian Army. Commanded from the end of October by Marshal Rodolfo Graziani, the Ligurian Army was charged with defending a line through the Western Alps from the Gulf of Genoa to the Franco-Italian frontier against Allied forces that had landed in southern France under Operation 'Dragoon'. It was also engaged in operations against partisans targeting German supply lines. The 5th Gebirgs Division fought under this formation until the end of the war, although various of its sub-units, notably the 100th Gebirgsjäger Regiment, were used to reinforce sectors of the line when breakthroughs threatened. Throughout the autumn the division held positions surrounding the plateau of Mount Cenis in Haut-Maurienne, preventing any attempt to break through the frontier and into Piedmont, behind the German armies from the Gothic Line. It was used variously to reinforce the 4th Alpine Division 'Littorio' in the Tarentaise sector, the Varese battalion on the Col du Petit-saint-Bernard, the Bergamo battalion on the Col du Tauchy and Col du Mont, and the Edolo battalion, which was being held in reserve. Facing them were three brigades of French Chasseurs Alpins, plus numerous irregular units such as the Francs Tireurs Partisans, Section des Eclaireurs Skieurs and Armee Secrete.

Through September and into October the US Fifth and British Eighth Armies continued to slog up the peninsula on roughly parallel lines of advance, using to full advantage the overwhelming air, armour and infantry firepower they now enjoyed in battles of attrition.

Rimini, gateway to the Romagna Plain, was finally taken by the Eighth Army on 21 September. Following this, British Empire forces pressed their attack northward, beginning a three-month operation known as the 'battle of the rivers'. On the Fifth Army front, the capture of the Il Giogo and Futa Passes ended the American phase of Operation 'Olive'. Advancing up Highway 65, by the end of September General Clark was in sight of the Po Valley and the snow-covered Alps beyond. Clark believed that both were now within his grasp, although winter weather now began to slow the advance to a crawl. Furthermore, German forces had inflicted heavy casualties on his troops and were still proving stubborn foes.

On 10 October, the US II Corps launched an assault against the ten-mile-long Livergnano Escarpment, a steep east–west line of solitary mountain peaks constituting Army Group C's strongest natural position in the northern Apennines. Here, as elsewhere, however, sustained Axis resistance, the exhaustion of the American troops, rugged terrain and poor weather halted the advance 10 miles south of Bologna.

Field Marshal Alexander now paused to consider another attempt at capturing Ravenna and Bologna, using the Fifth and Eighth Armies in concert. Meanwhile, across the lines, Kesselring's staff pressed their commander to fall back to the more easily defended Alps. Hitler however, facing Red Army gains on the Eastern Front and mounting pressures in northwest Europe, was loath to cede any territory voluntarily and ordered Kesselring to hold his current line. The field marshal, fearing to oppose the Führer, complied, placing two units from his reserve in front of II Corps.

In the last two weeks of October, the Allies rained hammer blows onto the German line, but all attempts to smash the defence and achieve a decisive breakthrough were fruitless. Instead the Fifth Army had to battle their way from mountain to mountain, while Polish, Canadian, Indian and British units of the Eighth Army fought north of Rimini in a continuation of the 'battle of the rivers'. On 27 October, General Sir Henry Maitland Wilson, the Supreme Allied Commander in the Mediterranean, ordered a halt to these offensives, citing Allied munitions and shipping shortages, troop exhaustion, the lack of replacements (largely due to the continued Allied emphasis on combat operations in northwest Europe and southern France and the priority given those areas in terms of manpower, munitions and supplies) and the ever more rapidly deteriorating weather conditions.

Field Marshal Alexander, still striving for an eleventh-hour breakthrough before winter, decided that another attempt on the German defences should be made by both armies with whatever strength they could muster. Eighth Army planners outlined another 'one–two punch', ordering its units to attack to the northwest toward Imola and Budrio, and north toward Ravenna and beyond. After 7 December or after the Eighth Army had taken Imola, whichever came first, Clark would launch the Fifth Army's assault with two divisions of II Corps.

Above: Gebirgsjäger in 1943-pattern reversible anorak armed with a StG44.

Left: The MP43 assault rifle was the forerunner of the modern day Kalashnikov. Cheaply produced from pressed metal it performed particularly well in the cold of Russia or the high mountains and was, therefore, prized by the Gebirgsjäger.

BATTLE GROUP 7

Battle Group 7
Staff 4th Alpini Division
Staff, 7th Mountain Regiment
III/7th Infantry Regiment
I/8th Infantry Regiment
II/5th Marine Infantry Regiment (from
    the 3rd 'San Marco' Marine Infantry
    Division)
II/4th Mountain Artillery Regiment
IV/4th Mountain Artillery Regiment
4th Engineer Battalion
4th 'Cadelo' Reconnaissance Group

The offensive began on schedule on 2 December, ending the two-month stalemate, but immediately ran into stiff enemy resistance from the 90th Panzergrenadier and 98th Infantry Divisions. Although the Canadian 5th Armoured Division entered Ravenna, a city liberated in large part by a massive uprising of Italian partisans on 4 December, Vietinghoff succeeded in stabilising his front along the Senio River, 10 miles farther north, and repulsed all subsequent attacks launched by Canadian, Polish, Indian and New Zealand units. When it was reported that the Germans had not reduced their strength in II Corps' area as anticipated, Alexander decided on 7 December to postpone further Allied offensive operations, and the front temporarily quieted.

In December there were major reorganisations in both the Axis and Allied high commands. On 23 October Field Marshal Kesselring had been severely injured when his staff car collided with a towed artillery piece on a crowded mountain road; the lengthy recuperation required effectively ended his tenure as Axis commander in Italy. Although he returned to duty in late January 1945, in early March Hitler gave him command of Army Group B in Western Europe, replacing Field Marshal von Rundstedt. General Vietinghoff commanded Army Group C until transferred to the Eastern Front in late January, and then returned to permanently replace Kesselring in March 1945. General Lemelsen stood in for Vietinghoff in the Tenth Army until 17 February 1945, when he was replaced by Generalleutnant Traugott Herr. At Fourteenth Army, Generalmajor Fridolin von Senger und Etterlin replaced Lemelsen before relinquishing command to Generalleutnant Kurt von Tippelskirsch, who in turn gave Lemelsen his old command back in February.

In the Allied camp, Wilson went to Washington as chief of the British Military Mission. Alexander succeeded him as Supreme Allied Commander in the Mediterranean and General Clark took command of the Fifteenth Army Group in place of Alexander. Major-General Lucian K. Truscott, Jr., returned from France to head the Fifth Army. General Sir Richard L. McCreery, who had replaced General Leese as Eighth Army commander on 1 October, remained in command of that force.

5TH GEBIRGSJÄGER WAR SERVICE

Dates	Corps	Army	Army Group	Area
10.40	Forming	Wehrkreis XVIII	–	Home
11.40–2.41	XVIII Corps	Second Army	Army Group C	Home
3.41–10.41	XVIII Corps	Twelfth Army	–	Greece, Crete
11.41	Recuperating BdE	Wehrkreis V	–	Home
12.41–3.42	BdE	Wehrkreis VII and XVIII	–	Home
4.42	I Corps	Eighteenth Army	Army Group North	Leningrad, Volkhov
5.42–7.42	L Corps	Eighteenth Army	Army Group North	Leningrad, Volkhov
8.42	XXVIII Corps	Eighteenth Army	Army Group North	Leningrad, Volkhov
9.42	XXVI Corps	Eighteenth Army	Army Group North	Leningrad, Volkhov
10.42	XXVI Corps	Eleventh Army	Army Group North	Leningrad, Volkhov
11.42	XXX Corps	Eighteenth Army	Army Group North	Leningrad, Volkhov
12.42–3.43	LIV Corps	Eighteenth Army	Army Group North	Leningrad, Volkhov
4.43–11.43	XXVI Corps	Eighteenth Army	Army Group North	Leningrad, Volkhov
12.43	Reserve	Tenth Army	Army Group C	Upper Italy
1.44–5.44	XIV Corps	Tenth Army	Army Group C	Italy (south of Rome)
6.44–7.44	LI Corps	Tenth Army	Army Group C	Italy
8.44	Reserve	Ligurian Army	Army Group C	Western Alps
9.44–4.45	LXXV Corps	Ligurian Army	Army Group C	Western Alps

Left: Wearing the 1943-pattern reversible anorak snow-side outwards, a reconnaissance team watches for the enemy.

OPERATION '*WINTERGEWITTER*'

On 26 December 1944, Axis forces launched Operation '*Wintergewitter*' (winter storm), a limited attack against the inexperienced 92nd Division of the US IV Corps, some 20 miles north of Lucca. Their forces, however, advanced only a few miles beyond Barga, before beginning a withdrawal on 27 December, and in four days of intense fighting in bitter weather they were pushed back to their original positions.

In early January 1945, the Allied commanders in Italy ceased large-scale military operations, to prepare for a new offensive scheduled for 1 April 1945. Despite two months of planning, limited offensives, and much manoeuvring, the Allied units came to rest on a winter line that had changed very little since late October 1944. Early in the year Clark decided to launch three small attacks to obtain the best possible starting points for the planned spring offensive, and achieved some small incremental gains. Except for these limited advances, the Allies contented themselves with resting, receiving reinforcements and stockpiling munitions, especially artillery shells and other supplies. As spring approached, the fully rested and resupplied Fifteenth Army Group prepared to renew the offensive in a campaign that most anticipated would take it into the Po Valley and mark the final Allied push of the war in Italy.

Axis forces, having successfully held the Gothic Line through the autumn and early winter, also used the lull to rest and refit, and attempted to strengthen their fallback positions. Although Vietinghoff's front still stretched from sea to sea, his military situation was deteriorating rapidly. Behind his lines, bands of Italian guerrillas harassed what remained of his bomb-shattered transportation system, setting roadblocks and blowing up railway tracks. From January 1945, the 50,000 tons of supplies that normally arrived each month from Germany ceased altogether, and his troops were forced to live off the land.

On 18 January, Generalmajor Hans Steets assumed command of the 5th Gebirgs Division, becoming its penultimate commander. Attempts were made to reinforce the badly depleted division with elements of the Italian 4th Alpini 'Monte Rosa' Division. This was divided into two elements, Battle Groups 7 and 8, and in February–March 1945, Battle Group 7 was parcelled out between the 5th Gebirgs Division and the 2nd Grenadier Division 'Littorio'.

ADVANCE TO THE ALPS

In April 1945, the months of inching progress through mud and mountains came to an abrupt end, when the US Fifth and British Eighth armies erupted into the Po Valley. Within three weeks the campaign in Italy was brought to a decisive end, as the now numerically vastly superior Allied forces raced to the Alps. But even as these last actions were played out, in the Western Alps there were further heroics from the men of the 5th Gebirgs Division.

The Battle of Mount Froid

In April 1945, the III Battalion of the 100th Gebirgsjäger Regiment and a company of the Italian Fascist Folgore Regiment occupied a key sector in the northwest of the Plateau du Mount Cenis in the Haut-Maurienne. In all they numbered about 1,500 soldiers with 20 howitzers and several heavy mortars. In the valley below them were three chasseurs alpins battalions of the 27th French Mountain Division, mostly composed of former maquisards. These 3,000 volunteers, although inexperienced and poorly equipped, were supported by 45 field guns.

On 5 April 1945, cloaked by a bitter wind and icy snow, the three French battalions facing the 5th Gebirgs Division on the frontier launched an offensive against the plateau of Mount Cenis, which controls access to the Suse Valley and Piedmont. The first target was Mount Froid, a peak 8,500 ft tall that commanded the valley and formed the cornerstone of the German stronghold. Its summit, a narrow ridge 2,100–2,400 ft long, was shielded by three strong points: the east and west blocks with two tumbledown casemates and a centre block with a network of trenches. Although the Gebirgsjäger fought back stoutly under a withering barrage of French artillery fire, the 4th Company of the XI Chasseurs Alpins battalion succeeded in conquering the middle and the western strong points. The next day, after a fourth attack, the same unit seized the eastern block, and Mount Froid fell into French hands.

Above: MG34 team wearing the winter reversible suit field grey side outwards.

In the course of 6 April, the French brought fresh troops and ammunition through the deep snow to the fog-shrouded mountaintop positions. Shortly before midnight, after a violent bombardment, a detachment of one German company and two Italian platoons, in five assault groups, approached the eastern casemate in a howling wind. While three groups made a frontal attack, the two others moved to outflank the position. The French garrison was quickly overwhelmed and, facing annihilation, took refuge in the centre block. The assault groups came on again, charging the casemate with submachine guns and hand grenades. The French chasseurs alpins defended themselves energetically, driving back first one then another assault. As dawn began to break on the exposed slope, the attackers were forced to retire.

After three failed counterattacks, German commanders resolved to evacuate the sector but Vietinghoff, fearing an Allied breakthrough to Turin in his rear, overruled them and ordered the 5th Gebirgs Division to recapture Mount Froid at any price. Reinforced by other elements of the division, the troops retook the position on 12 April. It was, however, to prove a hollow victory gained at a heavy cost. Two weeks later, Steets received orders to evacuate his men from the region.

On 20 April, Vietinghoff ordered the retreat, previously denied him by Hitler, to prepared positions on the Ticino and Po Rivers. That night, with defeat in Italy growing imminent, Gebirgsjäger of the 5th Gebirgs Division mounted one last defiant attack against the French VII Battalion Chasseurs Alpins' positions on Roc Belleface. Seven men made a night climb up the precipitous northeast wall of the mountain, and overcame the garrison's defences. It was a gallant act but, with the final battles in Berlin now being played out, ultimately futile.

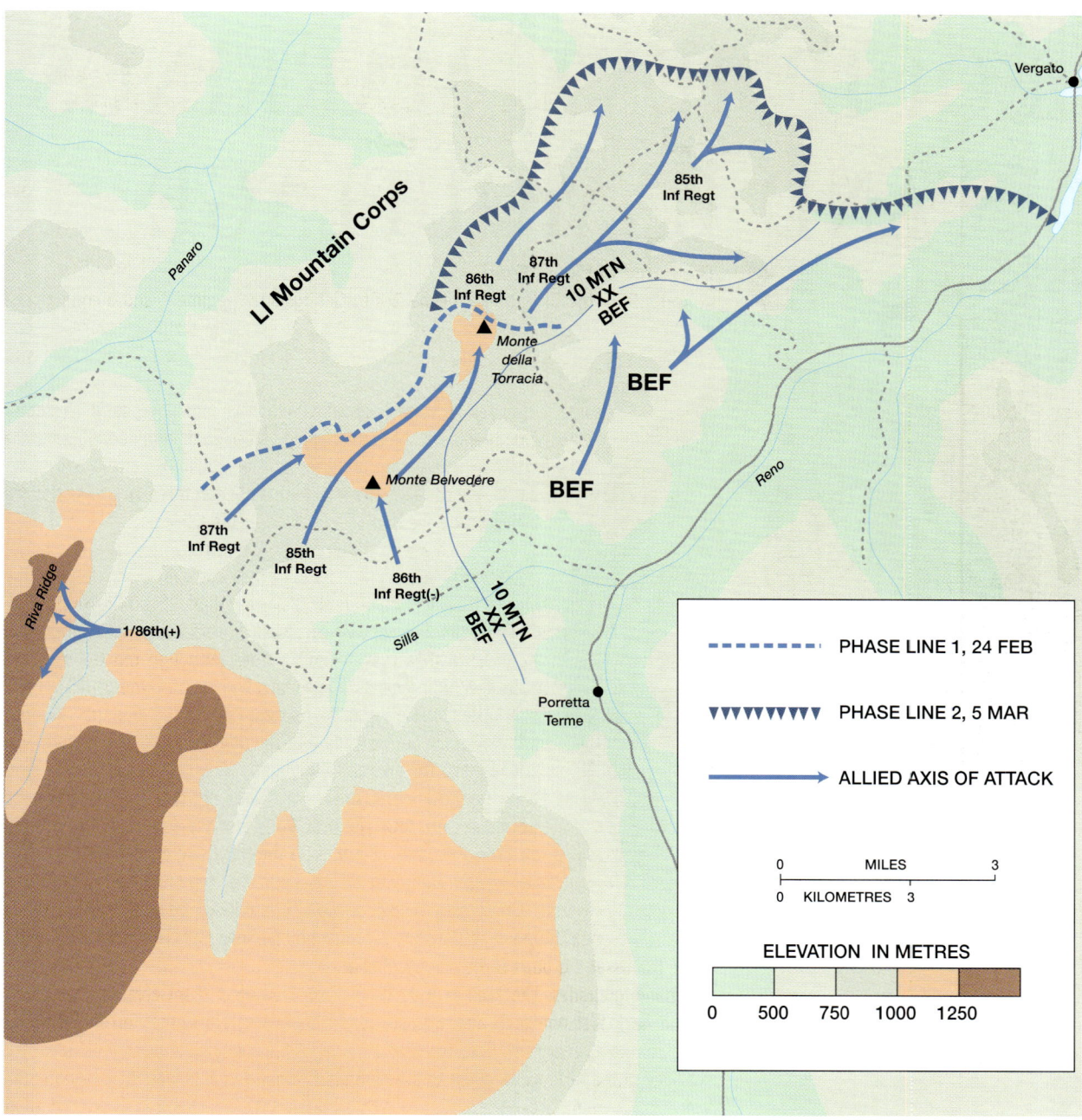

LI Mountain Corps

Panaro

85th
Inf Regt

87th
Inf Regt

86th
Inf Regt

10 MTN
XX
BEF

BEF

Monte
della
Torracia

Vergato

Reno

BEF

Monte Belvedere

87th
Inf Regt

85th
Inf Regt

86th
Inf Regt(-)

10 MTN
XX
BEF

Silla

Riva Ridge

1/86th(+)

Porretta
Terme

- - - - - - - - PHASE LINE 1, 24 FEB

ᐁᐁᐁᐁᐁᐁᐁᐁᐁ PHASE LINE 2, 5 MAR

⟶ ALLIED AXIS OF ATTACK

0   MILES   3
0   KILOMETRES   3

ELEVATION IN METRES

0   500   750   1000   1250

In the final days of April, the 5th Gebirgs Division continued to fight tenaciously, ignoring the inevitability of defeat. By now they were the last mountain division still fighting in high Alpine terrain. At the beginning of May, the division was regrouped for the last time and marched in full order eastwards toward Milan. During the journey there were skirmishes with Italian partisans, before the troops laid down their arms en masse to the US Fifth Army just north of Turin.

Above: The Allied Operation 'Encore' – 19 February to 5 March 1945.

EQUIPMENT, MARKINGS AND CAMOUFLAGE

Some basic details of the insignia, uniforms and equipment (including weapons) used by the 5th Gebirgs Division is provided below. For information on German army rank insignia, award badges and so on, refer to one of the many reference works on this subject listed in the bibliography.

INSIGNIA

The distinctive edelweiss insignia of both army and SS mountain units was based on a small white flower that grows exclusively in the high Alpine regions of continental Europe. It was first adopted under the Habsburgs in 1907 by the Austrian Landesschützen as their official unit insignia. In 1915 it was donated to the German Alpenkorps as a gesture of camaraderie, and from that time on it was worn on the troops' *Bergmütze* (mountain cap). After the First World War the edelweiss was used by a few Freikorps units, although in the Reichswehr only the soldiers of III Gebirgsjäger Battalion of the 19th Jägerregiment were allowed to wear it. On 2 May 1939, it was reintroduced as the insignia of all Gebirgstruppe in response to a request by General der Gebirgstruppe Ludwig Kübler to the OKH (Army High Command).

The 5th Gebirgs Division took as its divisional emblem the Gamsbock, a type of mountain goat noted for its agility on precipitous rock faces. The figurative representation of one of these animals was also used as a marking to distinguish divisional vehicles, and was one of the nicknames given to the division.

Above: Gebirgsjäger Edelweiss badge.

Right: Oberleutnant showing Edelweiss badge on right sleeve and left side of Bergmütze.

Below: The *Gamsbock* emblem of 5th Gebirgsjäger.

HEADGEAR

All ranks were issued with the standard German *Stahlhelm* (steel helmet) in either the 1935 or 1942 pattern, depending on their date of entry into service. Painted flat grey with no decals, this could be covered with a white 'winter' helmet cover. Gebirgsjäger were also issued with the standard German Army peaked cap (*Schirmmütze*) piped with the grass green Waffenfarben and with a small metal edelweiss worn between the national emblem and the wreathed cockade.

Away from the barracks and the parade ground, the mountain cap or *Bergmütze* was far more commonly seen was, and was highly prized by those who had won the right to wear it. Closely modelled on the cap worn by Austrian mountain units in the First World

War, this was produced in field-grey wool or tricot, and had a short peak and side flaps that could be folded down and fastened under the chin to protect the wearers ears and nape from the cold. The flaps were usually fastened at the front with flat green buttons. A cast-metal edelweiss insignia was worn on the left side, and on the front the national cockade and emblem. From 1943 this was replaced a new general issue field cap, based on the Bergmütze but with the longer peak of the tropical field cap. Also produced was a white camouflage cover.

Troops serving in the Mediterranean were issued with an olive-brown tropical field cap, with the same insignia as the Bergmütze. Until 1943 the national emblem and cockade were backed with an underlay of Waffenfarben, and even after this was discontinued many Gebirgsjäger continued the practice.

UNIFORMS

The general service dress of the Gebirgsjäger units followed the German Army standard. A four-pocket, grey, wool *Feldbluse* (field tunic) in either the 1941 or the simpler 1943 pattern was worn, with appropriate rank insignia and the embroidered edelweiss badge on the upper right sleeve. Collar and cuff patches, edelweiss insignia and officers' shoulder straps had an underlay of w*iesengrun* (grass green), the branch-of-service colour (*Waffenfarbe*) of the mountain troops. The same grass-green piping was applied to NCOs' and other ranks' shoulder straps, and to the front, collar, cuffs and trouser seams

Above: Cover of *Signal* magazine showing a mountain leader descending a rock face.

Right: 1941 view of Gebirgsjäger mountain artillery hauling their weapon by mule.

Left: Colour views from *Signal* magazine of rock-climbing training.

Below: Early war mountain troops rifle section ski patrol.

Left: This excellent portrait shows well the Edelweiss cap badge and 1939-pattern reversible anorak which was white one side, sage green the other.

Right: NCO wearing standard-issue greatcoat and Bergmütze.

Far Right: Windproof anorak suit issued 1943–4 to replace earlier types. It was white on one side, sage green the other.

Below: Gebirgsjäger in the two-piece winter suit pass PzKpfw IVs.

of walking-out dress. Finally, there was a grass-green strip in the centre of each officer's *Litzen* (collar patch), and on the earlier issues of NCOs' and other ranks' Litzen.

In addition, to the Waffenfarben, the following system of identification was used by Gebirgsjäger units on the shoulder straps and collar patches:

- Rifle and mountaineering units: unit number.
- Alpine and mountain troops school: gothic 'S'.
- Mountain troop divisional staff: embroidered 'D' with divisional number below.

Instead of the standard issue, field-grey, straight-legged trouser of the *Landser* (general infantryman), Gebirgsjäger were issued distinctive wide-cut mountain trousers (*Keilhose*), with reinforced seats and inside legs, tapered to allow them to be tucked into the boots.

For service in the Balkans and the Mediterranean theatres, Gebirgstruppen were issued with a regulation olive-coloured, cotton, four-pocket tunic, which could be worn with matching shorts, trousers or wider breeches. Puttees were usually discarded; instead socks were simply rolled down over boot-tops.

Winter clothing

Other standard items of clothing designed for use in cold climates, which were not exclusive to but used by the Gebirgsjäger, were the padded, reversible,

Below: Sighting for an MG42 gunner, this man wears a sage-green windproof jacket and has an ice pick and Bergen-style rucksack.

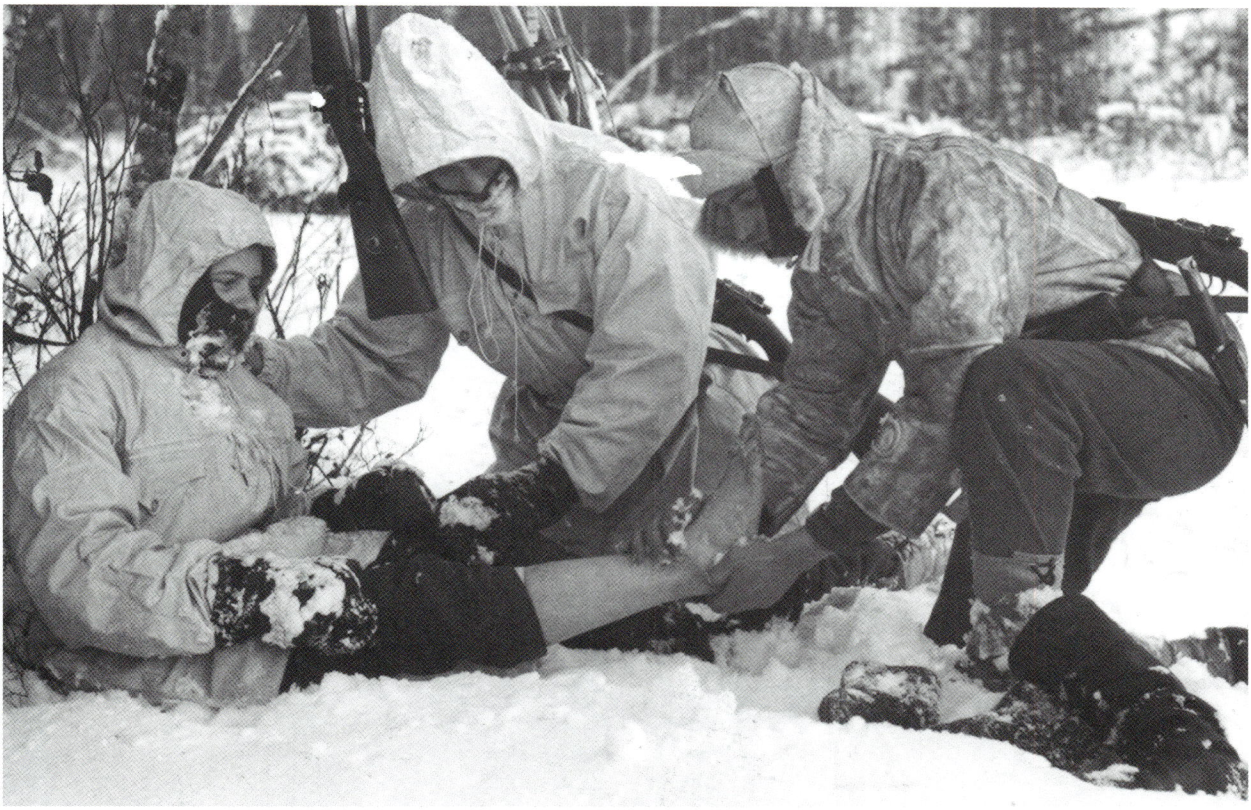

white/camouflage, hooded winter suit with matching mittens, a woollen balaclava to be worn under the helmet, standard army greatcoat, and felt overboots.

Unique to the Gebirgsjäger are the weighty (5 lb or 2.36 kg) ankle-length mountain boots and windproof jacket. The former had thick, studded and cleated leather soles, were fastened by eyelets and hooks, and could be worn with skis, crampons or snowshoes. In warmer climates a lighter boot was sometimes worn. The boots were topped with grey-green, woollen puttees (*Bergstiefel*) some 76cm long, fastened by a buckle and worn either to ankle or knee height. On occasion, canvas gaiters were preferred.

Also peculiar to the Gebirgsjäger was the sage-green *Windjacke* (windproof jacket) made from heavy-duty, close-woven calico, and designed to be worn over the field service blouse, primarily to cut wind-chill. It was double breasted with adjustable cuffs, a rear half-belt, skirt and 'muff' pockets, and provided some protection from the icy winds often experienced in mountains. The jacket could be worn over the belt with ammo-pouches. It had the same buttons and shoulder straps as the field service blouse, but some of the insignias were not worn on the *Windjacke*.

Above: First aid for an injured Gebirgsjäger – his rifle has been slung in the tree above. The men are wearing the 1939-pattern reversible anorak, white side outwards.

Below: The cuff-title 'Kreta' was instituted in 1942. (See next page.)

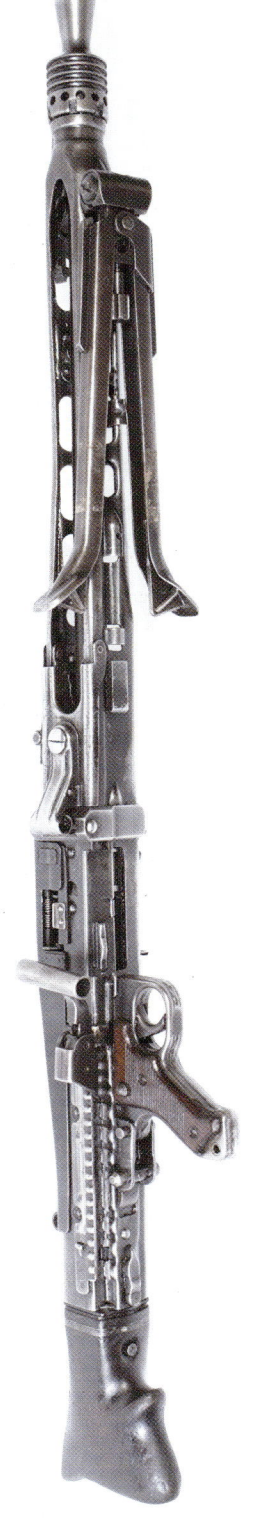

Right: MG34 with drum magazine.

Below right: MG42 gunner wearing sage green windproof jacket.

Below: Detail photograph of the MG42.

From 1942 a reversible, field-grey/white, hooded anorak with matching overtrousers was issued to the Gebirgsjäger. The cagoule-style, hooded anorak had a large flap to cover the neck opening, three breast pockets, a waist drawstring and a crotch strap that fastened to the front. The overtrousers had a drawstring waist. Neither item was particularly warm, and the anorak was generally less popular than the *Windjacke*.

Officers often wore privately purchased mountain caps, made of finer wool. Before 1942 there was no silver cord around the top on the mountain caps for officers, and only with the introduction of the field-cap Model 42 were officers allowed this distinction to their uniform. Generals wore a golden cord.

SPECIAL AWARDS

Along with the numerous awards for close combat, marksmanship, anti-partisan operations and the like issued to every branch of the services, men who had fought in the Narvik campaign in Norway were awarded a white metal shield bearing the legend 'Narvik 1940' (with an edelweiss for Alpine troops, or a propeller or anchor for Luftwaffe or Navy personnel). Of further interest is the Armelband Kreta, instituted in October 1942 for those men who had taken part in operations on Crete between 20–27 May 1941. Worn on the lower left sleeve, it was a white cloth band edged with golden-yellow Russia braid; in the centre was the embroidered legend 'Kreta', flanked with acanthus leaves. Far more rarely seen was the enamelled *Heeresbergführer* (army mountain leader) badge, worn on the left breast pocket and awarded only to those men, regardless of rank or age, who had achieved the highest level of mountaineering skill. This high-quality piece, keenly sought by collectors today, consists of an enamelled metal oval with a white outer border and green central field, surrounding an embossed silvered edelweiss with gilt stamens. At the base in gothic script is the title Heeresbergführer.

PERSONAL EQUIPMENT

This included all of the standard combat equipment of the German infantry along with other, more specialised kit. Standard equipment included a black leather belt with buckle, ammunition pouches, Y-shaped yoke straps of leather, a canteen, bread bag, bayonet, shelter (*Zeltbahn*), mess tin and cutlery, gas mask canister and entrenching tool. As bayonets, gas masks and helmets were too heavy for Alpine warfare, and of little worth, these were often left behind with the baggage train.

For operations in the high mountains the Jäger was issued with a 'Grosse' rucksack, the contents of which had to sustain him for days, weeks and often months. Inside the rucksack he carried his

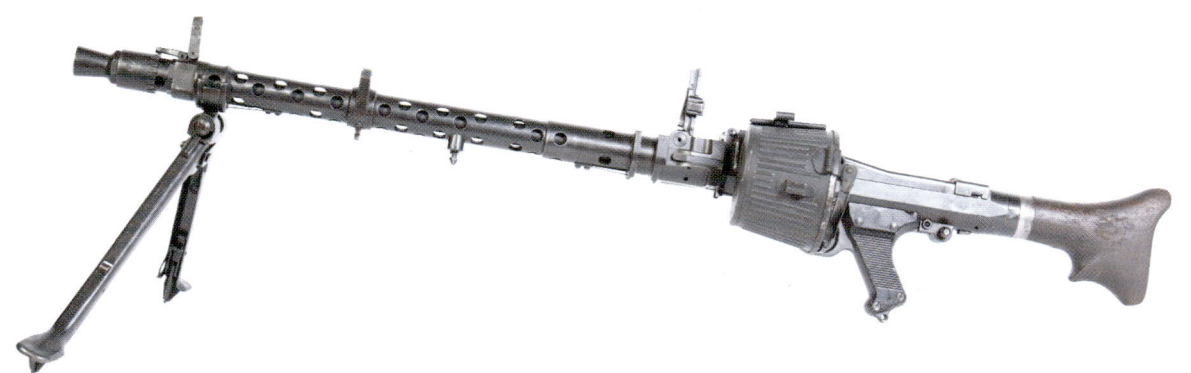

windcheater, spare shirt, spare trousers, spare socks, a groundsheet and woollen blanket. This last item proved less popular than the lighter, warmer and more compact Russian sleeping bag issued to Siberian troops, and examples of this were highly sought after. In addition, there was a Balaclava helmet, waist belt, gloves and the basic fighting ration: a kilo of bread (2.2 lb), one large tin of meat, and one small tin of lard. This had to satisfy dietary needs for two days, after which it was expected (but by no means guaranteed) that pack animals would bring supplies up to the front line.

To supplement this 'fighting ration', the troops were given a selection of high-calorie, low-bulk foodstuffs. Many calories were required to provide for the physical demands of marching and climbing in mountainous regions. These foodstuffs had to be edible either raw or very quickly cooked, since at high altitude the process of heating food requires more time and thus expends precious fuel. Air-dried meats, canned food, dehydrated vegetables and biscuits proved the best for these conditions, although on shorter operations chocolate, grape sugar or dried fruit were also practical. (Dried fodder for the pack animals was often provided in the form of cattle cake to avoid the problems of transporting bulky hay and grain.)

In his musette bag, the trooper carried an iron ration with chocolate and similar foodstuffs, washing gear, patching gear and candles or flashlight. In his blouse pockets he typically had two first-aid field dressings, a clasp knife, cigarettes, matches, pen and ink, and service pay book.

Platoon and section commanders (and runners) had to carry binoculars, message bags or signal pistols. The compass and binoculars were vital in the mountains and were issued right down to squad level.

MOUNTAIN EQUIPMENT

The Gebirgstruppe also had various specialised mountain equipment to hand, including skis, snow goggles, ice axe, a length of rope (three-eighths of an inch thick), the Grosse rucksack mentioned earlier, and ice hammer, crampons, snowshoes and pitons.

For traversing snow-covered terrain at speed, skis or snowshoes were essential, although both the army and the Waffen SS had their own Skijäger units. In icy conditions, crampons were used.

Snow goggles were standard issue as they provided protection for the eyes against harsh winds and were slightly tinted to protect against snowblindness. In the event that a snow storm, fog or darkness reduced visibility on the line of march, coloured ropes and flags were used to mark out a given route. Rope railings were employed for crossing crevasses in glaciers and were fitted with noise-making devices such as empty cartridge cases to aid orientation.

Rock-climbing equipment was issued to all Jäger units to suit their own personal requirements. Medical teams, for example, were issued with special stretchers that allowed the wounded to be lowered vertically down the side of a rockface. The medical teams had to deal with various types of injury, including snowblindness, frostbite and rope burns, which in some cases could be severe. Evacuation was almost always necessary in the case of severe injury, and ski stretchers were often employed for this task. These stretchers could be broken down and had folding legs, and in an emergency could be used as an operating table. Specially designed tents, some 16 ft in length, were employed to treat the wounded. They were made of light, windproof material and could be broken down into loads and transported by pack animals.

All told the average trooper was expected to be able to shoulder about 70 lb total weight, and be able to carry that over a vertical distance of rather more than 6,000 feet. However, as already mentioned it was impossible to fight with such a load, and the

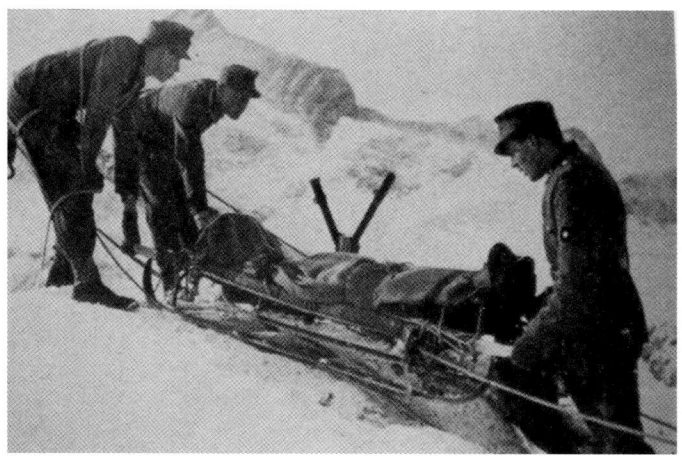

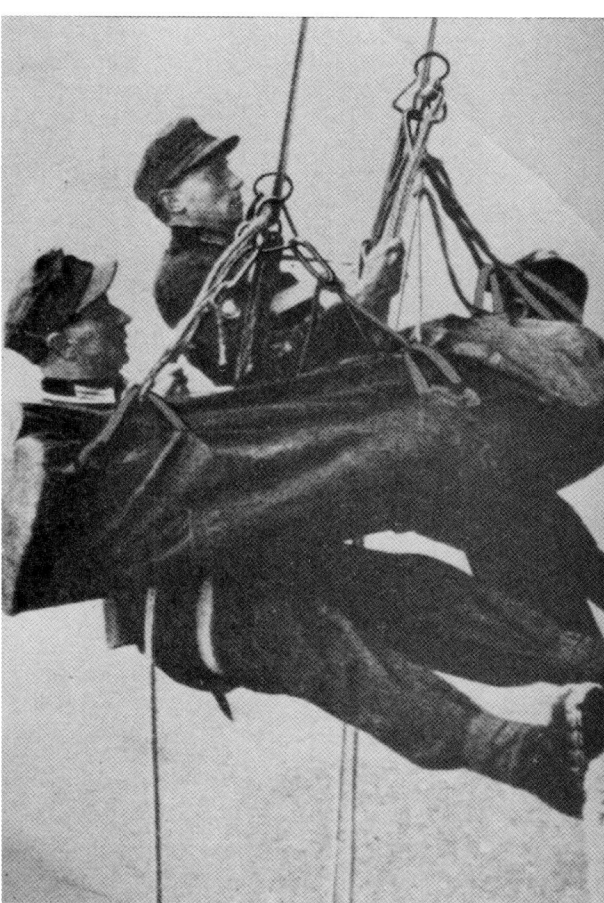

Above: Casualty evacuation on ski stretcher.

Left: MG15. Note folded bipod and stock.

Below: A tree trunk has been called into use with a block and tackle to haul a K15 gun to its firing position.

Right: Mountain stretcher of proofed canvas.

Below right: Specially designed MG34 snowshoe for front bipod legs.

Left: The 7.5cm Geb G36 – note wicker mats under wheels to give grip in snow. This weapon is emplaced at 18,400ft on Mount Elbrus, the furthest point of the German advance into the Caucasus.

Right: Kübelwagen towing a 37mm Pak 36 anti-tank gun. There were 12 of these weapons in each motorised anti-tank company.

Below: A 10.5cm leichte Feldhaubitze 16 – not specifically a mountain troops' weapon – being emplaced by Gebirgsjäger gunners in north Russia. Note the skid chassis for ease of handling in snow.

Grosse rucksacks were often laid down and brought up later from behind in the baggage train.

MOUNTAIN ARTILLERY

The light mountain artillery used by heavy companies and platoons in the direct fire support role was designed so that it could be fully dismantled and transported by pack animals to the fighting front. Trials with standard issue equipment had proved unsuccessful as the guns could not be broken down easily, so special equipment was introduced. As a rule, mountain artillery pieces had to be both light and very robust. Thus, different manufacturing techniques were devised. Extensive use was made of pressed parts rather than the more conventional machined parts.

To suit the specific needs of the mountain artillery, designs dating from the First World War were revised and updated, including the 75 mm (3 inch) Gebirgskanone (1915) and the 1918-vintage 75 mm leichte Gebirgskanone. A weapon based on the latter design was introduced in 1935. It weighed a little under 900 lb (400 kg) and had a range of rather over two miles (just over 3.5 km). Both remained in service until the end of the war. They were supplemented by the 75 mm Gebirgskanone 28 and, from 1938, by the 75 mm Gebirgsschütze 36 model, weighing in at 1,650 lb (750 kg) and capable of firing a 13 lb (6 kg) projectile to a maximum range of just over 5 miles (9.25 km).

Heavier fire support was provided by the *Gebirgshaubitze* (mountain howitzer) batteries. These used the 100 mm Gebirgshaubitze 16 or Gerät 77, and one of two 105 mm pieces. The Gebirgshaubitze 42, produced by the Austrian firm of Boehler did not reach the mountain artillery battalions until 1943–4. It weighed 1.66 tons, had a range of nearly eight miles (12.6 km), and could be broken down easily into four large parts to be towed by NSU Opel *Kattenkrad* (tracked motorcycle) in single axle carts.

Both German-made and captured guns were used. French guns included the 6.5 cm Gebirgskanone 221, the 7.5 cm Gebirgskanone 238 and the 10.5 cm Gebirghaubitze 322. Czech guns such as the 10 cm Gebirghaubitze, and the Russian 7.62 cm Gebirgskanone 307 were also adopted for use.

The mountain artillery regiments of the mountain divisions (in the case of the 5th Gebirgs Division, the 95th Gebirgs Artillery Regiment) also had the standard *schwere Infanterie Geschütze* (heavy infantry guns) and *schwere Feldehaubitze* (heavy field howitzer) of the German forces, for use in long-range fire support missions. Generally there was one battalion each of 105 mm and 150 mm howitzers. The 150 mm (6-inch) howitzer had a range of rather over eight miles (13.3 km), but due to its size and weight the heavy batteries had to operate on the lower slopes and valley floors, from where their support could be called on as required.

Below: 7.5cm light mountain gun IG 18 on the Russian Front in 1944.

INFANTRY WEAPONS

Kar 98k rifle
K/G43 semi-automatic rifle
MP40 submachine gun

Above: Artillerymen and mule team carry a K15 mountain gun to its position.

Left: Another view of the K15 mountain gun. The gunners are wearing calico wind jackets.

MP38/42 Beretta machine pistol
MP44
MG34 light machine gun
MG42 light machine gun
stick or egg grenades
P38 pistol
P08 pistol
G33/40 mountain carbine

In common with other branches of the infantry the standard issue rifle was the excellent Mauser Kar 98k, although large numbers of the so-called Gebirgskaribiner (Gewehr 33/40), a Czech-made variant of the Mauser with a shortened (46cm) barrel were also issued. As the distances at which combat took place could be considerable, these weapons were often equipped with either the zF41 (x 2.5 magnification) or zF4 (x 4 magnification) telescopic sights.

For close combat both the MP38 machine pistol and the MP40 submachine gun were used, primarily by squad leaders, and later in the war the semi-automatic Gewehr 43 and Sturmgewehr StG44 assault rifle were introduced in significant quantities. Captured examples of the simple yet tough and reliable Soviet PPSh-41 submachine gun were

Below right: Telefunken pedal power generator with signaller transmitting by morse key in the background.

Below: Funkgerät d2 radio set with three-man carrying team. The second man carries the battery pack.

highly prized. Officers carried either the Luger, P08 or, less frequently, Walther PPK automatic pistols.

In the squad support role the Gebirgsjäger used the ubiquitous MG 34 and later MG 42 light machine guns, both of which proved reliable in the harsh conditions of the mountains. With the aid of a mount that could be attached to either breech or barrel, it could be used as a fully automatic heavy machine gun or a light anti-aircraft weapon. Ammunition for the personal weapon was carried in belt pouches, and each man was usually also required to carry ammunition for the light machine guns.

Extensive use was also made of hand grenades for close quarter fighting, both the familiar stick pattern and smaller, egg-shaped *Eierhandgranate*. Light fire support

Above: Signaller laying field telephone cable from skis.

was provided by easily disassembled and transportable mortars, flak and light artillery. Particularly effective in the mountains, because of their high trajectory, were the mortars. The Gebirgs divisions used three main types: the 5 cm (2 inch) leichte Granatwerfer 36, 8 cm kurzer Granatwerfer 42, and 12 cm kurzer Granatwerfer 42. The 5 cm GrWf 36 was a sturdy little weapon weighing only weighing just over 30 lb (14 kg) and comprising just two basic components, a barrel and a base plate. It could fire a projectile weighing rather over 7.7 lb (3.5 kg) over 500 yards. From 1941 this was phased out in favour of the 8 cm (3 inch) kurzer Granatwerfer 42, which had more than double the range and nearly double the weight. This failed to live up to expectations and so from 1943 a 12 cm (4.75 inch) heavy mortar based on a Russian design was introduced.

The Gebirgs divisions also had dedicated anti-aircraft battalions equipped with a light 20 mm AA gun that could be broken down into eight major sub-components and be transported by pack animals. Towards the end of the war, this weapon proved particularly useful in defending the high passes of the Western Alps.

As in other units, the 5th Gebirgs Division's Panzerjäger (anti-tank) battalion was equipped with 37 mm L45 PAK 35/36, a weapon that proved wholly unsatisfactory against heavily armoured British and Russian tanks. Not until the introduction of the 50 mm gun did the situation improve.

COMMUNICATIONS

Given the lack of a transport infrastructure, communications in the mountains presented unique challenges. Radio transmitters were the principal means of communication over distance. Early sets included the Tornister Funkgerät, which weighed in at nearly 80 lb (35 kg) and required a three-man team to operate and transport it. Two of them carried the set – one the transmitter, one the batteries – and the other was the operator. This bulky set had a range of 2.5 miles (4 km) for voice, or 10 miles (16 km) sending a Morse signal. Later on in the war, much lighter radio equipment was developed, including the Feldfunk Sprecher B and C that could be carried and operated by one man.

Radio sets were issued right down to company level but could sometimes be rendered useless by high mountain peaks or atmospheric conditions that blocked their signals. Larger aerials were required than those used on conventional radio sets, and in an attempt to the combat the loss of signals experienced under certain atmospheric or topographical conditions, these were often attached to the tops of trees. Another tactic was to relay signals between stations. All of this equipment could be broken down into mule loads for transportation. A simpler and widely used method of signalling, and one less susceptible to interference, was semaphore. Provided visibility was good, a trained signaller could send messages to another man up to five miles away. Trained dogs were also used to send messages. (Large St Bernard dogs were also often employed to carry ammunition, food and medical packs, and were used by rescue teams.)

MOUNTAIN ENGINEERS

Within each Gebirgsjäger division there was a dedicated engineer battalion. As well as performing the normal combat engineer duties – mine-clearing, bridge laying, demolition and so forth – the *Gebirgspioniere* had numerous other tasks, among them improving mountain passes and roads by rock blasting, avalanche blasting and the draining of water from mountain roads. For these tasks they were equipped with the same tools and equipment as a regular infantry division and other more specialised kit. The Gebirgs engineer battalion could construct cable lines that could support loads of either 330 lb (150 kg) or 1,100 lb (500 kg) for moving men and equipment down from high areas. A difference in height of about 400 yards was required for them to be usable, and they could span an distance of 1,000 yards.

Below: Gebirgsjäger engineers repair a road to allow supporting StuG IIIs to advance.

Where roads were in poor condition or non-existent, new ones often had to be built. In the swampy areas around Leningrad, the engineers of the 5th Gebirgs Division were often called upon to build corduroy roads of logs so that vehicles could move through the cloying mud. Where a bridge had been blown, or simply did not exist, the engineers would be called on to construct anything from a simple rope walkway to a heavy pontoon bridge able to bear the weight of vehicles and heavy weapons. For this purpose, three types of bridging equipment were supplied to the Gebirgs engineer battalions. The Military (Mountain) Bridge Equipment G-Gerät kit provided the components to build a simple footbridge 120 yards in length, a 4-ton suspension bridge capable of supporting motor vehicles and horse-drawn carts, or a 2-ton inflatable-boat bridge that could span 60 yards. The B-Gerät kit enabled the construction of an 8–16-ton bridge supported by pontoon ferries; the K-Gerät was particularly useful in that it enabled the construction of a 20-yard-long, 16-ton bridge without assistance in only 20 minutes.

In addition, endless amounts of mines and mine-clearing equipment, snow probes, demolition explosives, detonators, electric and cordite fuses, power-saws, flame-throwers, rope and construction tools were required.

TRANSPORT

As mentioned earlier, when fighting in the mountains the Gebirgsjäger divisions were heavily reliant on the physical strength of their troops for logistics. At other times, when other assets could be employed, flexibility was important. In many cases, whatever was at hand would be pressed into service. The Gebirgstruppe in Lapland followed the example of the Finnish troops and used reindeer, while in the Caucasus Bactrian camels

Left: As has been shown aplenty in this book, the Gebirgsjäger used mules and horses to carry mountain guns and other equipment. Here the wheels of a K15 mountain gun are transported – note the handler (leading) has slung his rifle across his chest as per regulations.

Overleaf: A variety of means of transport for Gebirgsjäger – bicycles, skis, sledges, horses and Kettenkrads.

and small donkeys were pressed into service. The loads that these animals could carry were quite considerable, but without doubt the most widely used pack animals were mules and small sturdy ponies. Although in general mountain units were not fully motorised, two vehicles proved both suitable and popular in such terrain. These were the Kettenkrad tracked motorcycle, which could negotiate tight mountain passes and rocky terrain, and the light mountain car known as the *Erlkönig*, specially developed for the mountain units. It was light and fairly manoeuvrable while at the same time being quite robust. Artillery units had prime movers for their bigger weapons, but of course these were restricted to the roads, as were the plethora of other trucks and cars available to the units. Where there were no roads, lighter calibre artillery pieces had to be dismantled and drawn by animal teams on sleds, or else manhandled into position.

SHELTER

In the high peaks, access to some form of shelter from wind, rain and snow is vital given the constantly changing weather. On most occasions this had to be constructed by hand, and often very quickly. Men were taught how to dig caves in the ice or snow, and to make use of natural caves that were sometimes found on mountains. Finnish plywood shelters that could be broken down and transported, were often used, and proved effective as well as windproof. If a more permanent installation was required, the engineer units could throw up log cabins. The construction of mountain strongpoints and safety installations, with snow-fences and avalanche deflectors to guard against rock falls and avalanches, and fortified with barbed wire, was also the responsibility of the mountain engineer units. High winds often prevented conventional shelters from being constructed, however. In this case, simple stone walls were thrown up to act as windbreaks, behind which men could sleep.

PEOPLE

Right: 'Papa' Ringel.

JULIUS 'PAPA' RINGEL

Julius Ringel, or 'Papa' as he was known by his devoted men, was commander of 5th Gebirgs Division from its inception and during its most celebrated actions. Both charismatic and highly able, easily distinguished from most army officers by his goatee beard, Ringel was one of the best of the Gebirgstruppe commanders.

He was born on 16 November 1889 at Volkermarkt in Austria and in August 1909 joined the army. A year later he was a Leutnant with 4th Infantry Regiment and at the outbreak of was on the general staff (Ia) of the 3rd Gebirgs Division.

In August 1938, when the Austrian Army units were absorbed by the Wehrmacht, Ringel was promoted to Oberstleutnant. Now an officer in the German Army, three years later he was Oberst and a general staff officer (Ia) with 268th Infantry Division. At the end of October came his first command, 266th Infantry Regiment. Prior to the invasion of France Ringel was given his first divisional command, the still organising 5th Gebirgs Division. In early June, with the campaign mostly concluded, preparations began for the invasion of England ('Sealion') and for this Ringel was chosen to lead 3rd Gebirgs Division. He was returned to 5th Gebirgs Division when Operation 'Sealion', was cancelled and led it into the Balkans. His leadership on Crete won him the Knight's Cross, to which Oakleaves were added in 1943 after service on the Leningrad Front. After the division was transferred to Italy, in April 1944 he moved up to command LXIX Mountain Corps for a brief period. In June came promotion to General der Gebirgstruppe and commander of XVIII Mountain Corps. Finally, in February 1945, Corps Ringel was created. After the war he wrote an account of the 5th Gebirgs Division titled *Hurra! die Gamsbocks*, which remains its finest history. He died on 10 February 1967.

MAX-GÜNTHER SCHRANK

In February 1944 command of the 5th Gebirgs Division passed to Generalleutnant Max-Günther Schrank. Schrank was born in 1898 and died in 1960. He won the Knight's Cross in July 1941.

Above: Ringel decorates men of the division after the invasion of Crete.

HANS STEETS

Steets took comnand of 5th Gebirgs Division in Febuary 1945 and led it until succeeded by Karl Kurz.

KARL KURZ

Last of the commanders of the 5th Gebirgs Division, and the most short-lived, was Karl Kurz. He took command on 3 May 1945 and led it until the general surrender.

KNIGHT'S CROSS HOLDERS

Below is a complete list of Knight's Cross winners, and the date of the award, from 5th Gebirgsjäger Division.

Friedrich Bachmaier	9 January 1945
Max Burghartswieser	9 July 1941
Josef Ehinger	22 August 1943
Richard Ernst	20 October 1944
Albin Esch	13 June 1941
Albert Gaum	13 June 1941
Anton Glasl	11 October 1943
Franz Gnaden	8 August 1941
Josef Hampl	10 September 1943
Helmut Hermann	18 December 1944
Adolf Hofmann	15 November 1941
Franz Holzinger	13 April 1944
August Krakau	21 June 1941
Matthias Langmaier	29 February 1944
Franz Pfeiffer	13 June 1941
Franz Poeschl	23 February 1944
Heribert Raithel	13 June 1941
August Rappel	29 November 1944
Karl Riesle	29 February 1944
Julius Ringel	13 June 1941
Siegfried Rupprecht	10 September 1943
Johann Sandner	13 June 1941
Lorenz Schmied	29 November 1944
Max-Günther Schrank	17 July 1941
Leopold Schrems	27 July 1944
Otto Schury	17 July 1941
Egon Teeck	8 August 1941
Willibald Utz	21 June 1941
August Wittmann	21 June 1941
Hans Zwickenpflug	5 April 1945

Note: It worth noting that the first soldier of the Wehrmacht to be awarded the coveted Oakleaves to the Knight's Cross of the Iron Cross was a Gebirgsjäger, Generaloberst Eduard Dietl. His name was adopted by the Gebirgsjäger training school of the post-war Bundeswehr, the 'Dietl Kaserne'.

AUGUST WILHELM KRAKAU

One of the most celebrated 5th Gebirgs Division officers, Krakau was born on 12 September 1894, at Pirmasens in the Rhein-Pfalz, Bavaria. He volunteered for service at the outbreak of the First World War in August 1914, and a year later was promoted to Gefreiter. By the end of 1917 he was a Leutnant and deputy commander of the 1st Company of the Bavarian 2nd Jäger Battalion, and ended the war as commander of the 3rd Company of the Bavarian 2nd Jäger Battalion upon the demobilization in Germany.

After a spell as a militia leader, he joined the post-war Reichswehr and took part in the suppression of internal unrest in central Germany. During the 1920s and early 1930s he slowly climbed the promotion ladder until appointed commander of the II. Battalion/Infantry Regiment 41 of the 10th Infantry Division on 12 October 1937. In September 1939, the 10th Infantry Division took part in the invasion of Poland where it participated in the capture of Warsaw. In February 1940 he was commander of Infantry Regiment 85 of the 10th Infantry Division and took part in the invasion of France as a component of Generaloberst Wilhelm List's Twelfth Army.

On 5 October 1940 the 85th Infantry Regiment was redesignated the 85th Gebirgsjäger Regiment and assigned to the 5th Gebirgs Division, and under Krakau fought in the spring of 1941 first in Greece and then Crete. In May 1942, Krakau was delegated with the leadership of the 7th Gebirgs Division in Finland, which he led until captured in Norway on 9 May 1945. He died in January 1975 at Oberpfalz.

ASSESSMENT

Although far less publicised than the elite Panzertruppe, Fallschirmjäger and Waffen-SS, the Gebirgstruppen of the German Army deserve equal recognition.

By a considerable margin, 5th Gebirgsjäger Division was the best trained, led and motivated of the 10 mountain divisions within the German Army during World War II, and by some measure the best of any nation. It was certainly the only one used consistently in its intended role and environment. Although mountain troops are already reckoned something of an elite, within that small group 5th Gebirgsjäger Division has few peers.

In their very first combat, at the Metaxas line in Greece, 5th Gebirgsjäger Division men showed considerable mettle in breaching this fiercely defended, seemingly impregnable fortification. Following on from that, the speed with which they maintained the pursuit of the retreating British forces through the Greek mountains to the south coast is testimony to their hardiness.

In Crete, the division flew into a cauldron and put out the fire. Gambling all on a highly risky assault into Maleme while this was still under fire, the Gebirgsjäger can be credited for averting the disaster that otherwise would have befallen Student's Parachute Corps. And this despite suffering one of their own at the hands of the Royal Navy in the waters off the island, when the motley collection of boats that had been hastily collected together to transport them to the island was intercepted. Then, in driving the defenders across Crete into the sea, the division was able to demonstrate the abundant skills of mountain craft and physical endurance in rapid advances across difficult terrain.

In Russia, fighting a very different kind of war in the miserable swamps around Leningrad, these skills were largely wasted. Nevertheless, the division gave a good account of itself in the stagnant defensive battles on this front, acting in the role of a 'fire brigade' on the porous sectors.

Transferred to Italy, the division was again relegated to a defensive role. In the brutal battles on the Gustav Line at Cassino, and on the Gothic Line to the north, it mounted a tenacious defence despite merciless pounding by Allied aircraft and artillery, which helped frustrate Allied ambitions time and again and prevented them from redeploying units that could have shortened the war on other fronts. In the final months of the war, fighting once again in the mountains, this time on the Franco-Italian border, 5th Gebirgs Division successfully fended off attempts to break through to the rear of the retreating German Army.

It should be emphasised that for an infantry division, 5th Gebirgsjäger Division was comparatively lightly armed, and furthermore depended for mobility on its men and pack animals. Morale seems to have been consistently high, even under the most trying of circumstances. What is more, the problems with discipline that afflicted other lesser parts of the German army do not seem to have touched the 5th Gebirgsjäger Division, and it ended the war with honour intact. In final judgement, this truly was an elite.

REFERENCE

BIBLIOGRAPHY

Clark, Allan: *The Fall of Crete*; Cassell, 1962.
Excellent general description of the battle.

Clark, Mark: *Calculated Risk*; Harper, 1950.
Commander of Fifth Army gives the best war memoir on Italy.

D'Este, Carlo: *World War II in the Mediterranean, 1942–1945*; Algonquin Books/Chapel Hill, 1990.

Dunnigan, James F. (ed.): *The Russian Front: Germany's War in the East, 1941–45*; Arms and Armour, 1978.
Excellent general survey of the Eastern Front battles.

Fisher, Jr., Ernest F.: *Cassino to the Alps*; Washington Center Of Military History, 1977.
The most comprehensive work on the Italian campaign.

Forty, George: *Battle for Crete* and *Battle for Monte Cassino*; Ian Allan Publishing, 2001, 2004.
Two heavily pictorial surveys of these important battles.

Gordon-Douglas, S. R.: *German Combat Uniforms 1939–45*; Almark, 1970.
The focus of this book is on combat equipment and field uniform.

Hogg, Ian: *The Encyclopedia of Infantry Weapons of WW II*; Regent Books, 1984.
A fully comprehensive, illustrated work, including every type of weapon used by every army in the Second World War.

Keegan, John (ed.): *Encyclopedia of World War II*; Bison Books, 1977.
A short, many-sided history of the war as a whole. It includes biographies, details of major weapons, weapon systems, and details of all major battles.

Kaltenegger, Roland: *Weapons and Equipment of the German Mountain Troops in World War II*; Schiffer, 1995.
Largely pictorial record of the German mountain troops with brief details of their organisation.

Lucas, James: *Alpine Elite*; Jane's Publishing Company, 1980.
Lucas, James: *Hitler's Mountain Troops: Fighting at the Extremes*; Cassell, 1999.
Merriam, Ray: *Gebirgsjäger: Germany's Mountain Troops*; World War II Journal, No. 9.
Three good surveys of the Gebirgsjäger.

Mitcham, Samuel W.: *Hitler's Legions*; Cooper, 1985.
The organisation and technical aspects of the German divisions are described. Every part of the army is covered.

Mitcham, Samuel W.: *Hitler's Field Marshals*; Guild Publishing, 1988.
Biographies of the German field marshals and accounts of their major battles.

Orgill, Douglas: *The Gothic Line, Autumn 1944*; Heinemann, 1967.
Good detailed battle history.

Purnell-Hart/Pitt (eds): *History of the Second World War*; Purnell, 96 parts, published weekly during the 1960s.
Written in the main by the soldiers themselves, this is a real trove of information.

Williamson, Gordon: *German Mountain and Ski Troops 1939–45*; Osprey, 1996 and *Gebirgsjäger – German Mountain Trooper 1939–45*; Osprey, 2003.
Two classic Osprey equipment titles.

WEBSITES

http://www.Gebirgsjäger.4mg.com/
Currently the most detailed source of information on the German mountain troops currently available on the web.

http://www.geocities.com/Gebirgstruppe/index-e.html
'The mountain troops of the Wehrmacht.' Good colour pictures of uniforms, and details of divisional markings.

http://www.kameradenkreis-Gebirgstruppe.de/
Kameradenkreis der Gebirgstruppe E.V. In der Internationalen Föderation der Gebirgssoldaten (IFMS). German language site of the German Gebirgsjägers past and present. Also honours the mountain soldiers of other nations.

http://www.thirdreichruins.com
Has a picture of the Gebirgs memorial at the Gebirgsjäger barracks.

http://www.feldgrau.com
Excellent site providing detailed information and statistics on the German armed forces during from 1919–45.

http://www.axishistory.com/
Axis History Factbook. Another excellent site, still under construction, providing detailed information and statistics on the German armed forces from 1919–45. Currently one of the most detailed online sources of information on the Third Reich.

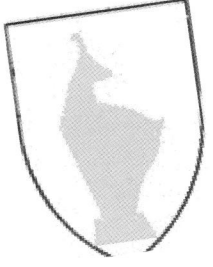

http://www.onwar.com/maps
Campaign maps from the Second and other wars.

http://www.tankclub.agava.ru/sign/sign.shtml
Russian-language site with excellent illustrations of the tactical signs of the German Army.

RE-ENACTMENTS

5th Gebirgsjäger 100th Regiment 1st Battalion 2nd Company Virginia-based living history unit with members from VA, MA, NY.
Email: scvoli@aol.com

1./Gebirgsjäger.Regiment 98.
US-based living history unit who can be contacted via:
http://www.reenactor.net/units/gjr98/1-gjr98-home.html

FURTHER RESEARCH

Bundesarchiv – Militärarchiv
Federal Records Office – Military Archive
Postfach, 79024 Freiburg
Wiesenthalstrasse 10
D-79115 Freiburg
Deutschland

Bundesarchiv – Zentralnachweisstelle
Federal Central Record Office
Historical records office of the German Federal Republic. Available upon application for use by researchers and authors.
Bundesarchiv-Zentralnachweisstelle
Abteigarten 6

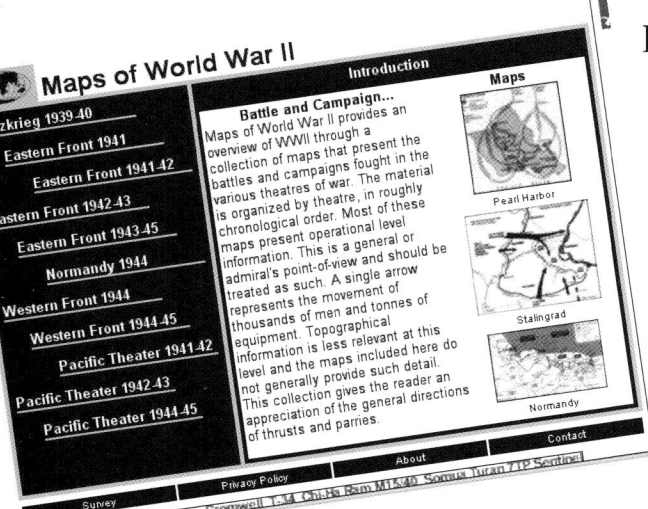

D-52076 Aachen
Deutschland
http://www.bundesarchiv.de

Bundesarchiv-Personalarchiv
Federal Records Office – Personnel Archives
Information on personnel questions relating to Second World War survivors.
Bundesarchiv-Personalarchiv
Abteigarten 6
D-52076 Aachen
Deutschland

Bundesministerium der Verteidigung
Ministry of Defence
Bundesministerium der Verteidigung
Postfach 13 28
D-53003 Bonn

Deutschland

Verband des Krieges
German War Veterans Organisation
Verband des Krieges
Wurzerstrasse 2-4
D-53175 Bonn
Deutschland

Volksbund Deutsche Kriegsgräberfürsorge
German War Graves Commission
Maintains German war graves all across the world. Has a database of fallen or missing German soldiers, with the location of their graves (if known).
Volksbund Deutsche Kriegsgräbefürsorge
Werner-Hilpert-Strasse 2
D-34112 Kassel
Deutschland
http://www.volksbund.de/homepage.htm

Arbeisgemeinschaft für Kameradenwerke und
Traditionsverbaende e.V
Kameraden Veterans Magazine
The official newsletter for German Second World War veterans.
Arbeisgemeinschaft für Kameradenwerke und
Traditionsverbüde e.V
Tuebinger Strasse 12-16
D-70178 Stuttgart
Deutschland

MEMORIALS

At the Gebirgsjäger barracks in Berchtesgaden-Strub, Bavaria, in Germany is a memorial to German mountain troops of the Second World War. It takes the form of a lion mounting a peak, which itself stands on a stone plinth.

INDEX